CONCILIUM

Religion in the Seventies

CONCILIUM

Concilium 129 (9/1979): Spirituality

MODELS OF HOLINESS

Edited by

Christian Duquoc
and
Casiano Floristán

THE SEABURY PRESS/NEW YORK

1979
The Seabury Press, 815 Second Avenue, New York, N.Y. 10017
ISBN: 0-8164-2037-8 (pbk.)   0-8164-0130-6

T. & T. Clark Ltd., 36 George Street, Edinburgh EH2 2LQ
ISBN: 0-567-30009-9 (pbk.)

Library of Congress Catalog Card Number: 80-65211
Printed in the United States of America

CONTENTS

Editorial

THE CATHOLIC CHURCH does more than administer the temporal forms of the kingdom of God, it elevates to eternal glory those who have served it on earth: it canonises. There have been many historical variants of the official declaration of sanctity. For a long time access to heavenly glory was decided by the spontaneous sentiment of the Christian people, and there was no question of legal criteria and canonical procedures. Most saints on the calendar have not been submitted to the processes of Rome. When the Church became more organised, however, and acquired a legal system, it felt itself obliged to pass laws about the official passage into the hereafter. In so doing, it produced models of holiness, because, even if all are called to enter the kingdom of heaven, not all have the honour of doing so officially. To gain official entry on the basis of the record of achievement in the Church on earth (and nobody has yet thought of canonising a non-Catholic believer, although nobody restricts the kingdom of God to Catholic believers alone) is a matter of having matched up with a certain notion of holiness prevalent among the Catholic people or the courts in Rome. The Church elevates to the kingdom of God those who serve her, but does serving her always amount to promoting the kingdom of God in this world?

The present issue deals with models of holiness. We are not concerned exclusively with 'models' that have emerged from the process of canonisation, although these have a quite special weight on account of the way in which the community of the Church and the authority of Rome are involved. The Catholic faithful have other models of holiness offered to them by methods of spirituality, by traditions of religious and monastic orders or by the demands of individual service of other people's policies. So articles in this issue study these aspects. At the same time it was necessary to scrutinise closely the procedure for the official determination of sanctity and the models produced by this determination. It is, of course, not a question of the spiritual and subjective power of holiness but of its social form. Some people may well think that we are concentrating on a purely formal aspect of holiness. That may be so, but that is what gives this issue its shape. And the choice of this point of view allows us to discern practical, historical and theoretical criteria of holiness. Heaven does not escape from the relativity of our social perceptions.

The problems surrounding this subject are complex. The relationship between the ideal or the imperative and the social reality of the Church raises certain serious theological questions which I summed up a little higher up by asking: Does the Church elevate to official sanctity those who have served it, or rather those who have served the coming of the kingdom? We shall see further on that these two ends are not identical on account of the fact that the Catholic Church is a social reality that is not always governed by the interests of the Gospel alone. 'Be holy because I am holy', says the Lord in the Old Testament, and this command punctuates the moral law of the first Bible. 'Be perfect as your heavenly Father is perfect', says Jesus in the Sermon on the Mount, and this ideal determines the whole style of evangelical life.

These imperatives are clear enough at the level of a general theory of imitation of divine action, but they become more obscure as soon as they become guidelines for daily living. Nobody has ever seen God, and nobody had better put himself in his place in order to define the ways in which holiness should be realised concretely in the world. Models are born out of the space created between the imperative and concrete action. The imperatives already mentioned need to be mediated in order to become effective. A model is for imitation, it works upon the imagination, it charms the affections, whereas an imperative or a demand leaves one undecided about the way to realise it concretely. Models were a method of making the imperatives of the Old Testament or the demands of the Gospel relevant and attractive or heroic.

A model does not, however, depend only on the imperatives and demands of the Gospel; it bears the imprint of the interests, the social gambits and the prejudices of the Church of its time. This is the way in which the Church has canonised as martyrs (e.g., St Peter of Verona) inquisitors assassinated by people charged with heresy. It overlooks the fact that the Inquisition was an odious and immoral institution which did not baulk at using lying techniques and torture—things that do not seem to be specially evangelical. In fact we can e surprised and even shocked that the Church did not canonise a single person who protested against the methods of the Inquisition which have done so much harm to the church in Europe and which still weighs it down today. A recent debate on French television about an Italian film on Giordano Bruno, a Dominican burned at the request of the Roman Inquisition, showed how distrustful many people are about the exhortations of the Church in favour of the rights of man. One of the participants in the debate said that Himmler and Lenin industrialised the techniques described in the manual of the inquisitors. It is, therefore, not at all clear that those who served the immediate interests of the Church in the Inquisition and who were canonised by the Church for their pains really served the interests of the Gospel.

The case of the Inquisition is not the only thing to give rise to questions. The history of those put forward as models of holiness has other surprises in store for us: Why is it that so many monks, virgins, widows and bishops people official heaven; whereas layfolk, married women and ordinary priests are hardly represented there at all? Representations of heaven in the art of the Middle Ages or of the renaissance reproduce the social hierarchies which obtained within the Church: the peasant does not sit at the side of the pontiff. The virgins remain grouped together, there is no question of mixing them up with the rest of the population. It is only in representations of hell that this hierarchy is contravened: bishop and highway brigand jostle each other. A suspicion begins to arise: Does not the procedure of canonising somebody in the light of models of holiness that are in some sense predetermined reveal more about the ideal of an epoch than about the demands of the Gospel?

To throw light on the social infrastructure of given models of holiness does not condemn the Catholic faithful to scepticism. Evangelical holiness is not a chimera and canonisations have not peopled heaven with personalities useful to the powerful of this world or to the churches. We do, however, have to challenge a view we take too much for granted, namely, that holiness is an absolute type that can be transcribed into social categories. No, models are relative and do not exhaust the forms of Christian holiness. We have to resituate this holiness within the totality of the Christian population and orientate ourselves not so much by official norms as by the one norm that escapes all criteria: Jesus of Nazareth whom we confess to be holy.

Jesus refuses to go along with the claim to establish norms and criteria of holiness made by religious tribunals. His experience testifies to the danger of arrogating to oneself judgement on fidelity to God. The enlightened Jews of his time did not lack criteria of holiness: they could be plotted socially in terms of the law. Not, of course, that anybody was stupid enough to think that material fidelity to the law was sufficient to constitute accomplishment of the will of God. The law nevertheless remained in practice the ultimate criterion. Jesus was not well adjusted to these religious and social criteria because he put up no resistance to examination on the part of those who knew and applied the law. The experts in religion did not see a man of God in him whom the Christian tradition has recognised as being in every way one of us except in regard to sin; in fact they saw in him a blasphemer. Now it would be unjust to accuse his adversaries of villainy or hypocrisy. I should prefer to say myself that they were upright, but limited; virtuous, but narrow; rigorous, but fussy; incapable of imagining other parameters of behaviour than those that corresponded to their ideal. Narrowness of spirit coupled with sincere and uncompromising virtue is one of the principal causes of crime in the world. History is crowded with virtuous people who were a menace to their kind. Jesus was condemned by virtuous men, not by the debauched and the infamous. Virtuous men ran the Inquisition. This tragic misunderstanding at the very start of Christian history, this inability to bring together strict virtue and the holiness coming from God, reappears within Christian communities themselves. Their attempts to encourage evangelical holiness have too often served only to try virtue and have made the world a sadder place. Life lived according to the models of holiness proposed by some forms of spiritual guidance would be life without savour, relish or creativity. Nietzsche wanted a God who danced—such a God would not look much like the promotors of saintly virtue. But if Jesus fitted uneasily into pre-established categories, Mary is a different case. The return to the Jesus of history has been the recurrent source of challenge to established criteria. Can one say the same for Mary? The Gospel tells us little enough about her, except that she was a believer, just and the mother of Jesus. She put all her trust in God, like Abraham. Unfortunately, this was not the aspect of her that was emphasised, and especially not in popular piety. It has been more Mary's social roles as virgin and mother that have caught the attention than her faith.

Mother: this title allows for the exaltation of the woman's role as mother and for the demonstration that it is in taking on this role fully, even to the point of complete abnegation and renunciation of all social power, that women enter upon a divine path.

Virgin: this quality encourages the neutralisation of the originally sexual character of maternity, tied as it is to the relationship of husband and wife. It invests non-conjugal life with value as a Christian form, whilst retaining the family and social advantage of the conjugal life evoked by the other title.

In this way, the holy family (for this is the only one that is called holy) can glorify an institution necessary for the balance of society at the same time as it puts to one side the affective harmony and delight of the couple that could offset the ascetic ideal of happiness. Amongst the people, and sometimes even officially, Mary's social roles, which are contradictory in themselves, make a singular, unapproachable and yet fascinating person of her since she realises within herself what no Christian woman can realise simultaneously. Mary is a model because she gives value to feminine roles, and yet she is a model that can be imitated only by the renunciation of maternity. In this way she helps to keep the ordinary Christian in second place. The inflation of these two roles of Mary as wife and virgin is compensated by the lack of interest shown in just what does make Mary a saint: her faith, a model that is relevant to all Christians, even if the implications are not concretely obvious. But this faith did not warrant the sacralisation of a double feminine role; on the contrary, it relativised them both by compelling them to be thought and lived humanly and not divinely. What is important is not that Mary is a virgin, nor that she is a mother, but that she believed, like Abraham. These other two qualities become meaningful only in the light of her believing obedience to the Word of God.

Jesus and Mary are inimitable models, but for incommensurable reasons: Jesus, because he did not conform to any predetermined criterion of holiness, because he was in this way altogether creative. He is not a model that can be canonised. From this point of view, it would be interesting to study the holiness of Jesus in comparison with other historic forms in the Church. Nietzsche grasped the extraordinary originality of the Nazarene very well. Mary is inimitable because she takes on two contradictory feminine roles. In order to make her imitable, one has to define her as a believer but in so doing one automatically relativises the ambiguous function of sacralising the feminine roles which we have made her fulfil. This is why Jesus is the pre-eminent icon of holiness, because he distances all models, and it is in this respect that he alone is the holy one. Mary is inimitable in so far as one does not allow her two roles as mother and virgin to be questioned by the Gospel. She is imitable as a daughter of Abraham the believer, but in that case she stops being a sacred model, functioning socially in such a way as to justify eternal feminine roles. For women in effect do not enter the official heaven unless they are virgins or widows. 'Widows' is the only way of alluding to the fact that they are mothers, neutralising as it does the importance of the conjugal bond for the purposes of entry into the official heaven. This fascination with the humanly contradictory status of Mary is all the more surprising as the Gospel utterances about her flatter neither the institution of the family nor the status of mother, but only faith. This last fact could not find social expression any more easily than Jesus' life-style, and that is why it has remained in the shadow. In other words, the relevance of Jesus and Mary to the appreciation of official Christian holiness justifies the inclusion of two articles about them in an issue on models of holiness.

Such being the difficulties surrounding the cases of Jesus and Mary, they must be passed on to the Catholic faithful, even if they become different in degree or in kind in the process. The articles on the 'canonisation of saints and its social operation', on 'hagiographic variations on the theme of Mother Agnes of Jesus', on 'models of popular holiness' and on 'models of priestly holiness' will surely convince the reader that the turbulent history of our existence and our Church resonate in the calm of eternal bliss. It is true that canonised saints have not gone so far as to meet the fate of the heroes of some countries, glorified today, disgraced tomorrow. The saints in heaven need fear only changes in popularity or shifts in liturgical esteem. With the lapse of time, they run the risk of

coming down in the world of Church and popular piety; they even risk
becoming secularised. This need not shock us. Real people or methods
are ways, but they can also be obstacles in the path of understanding
evangelical holiness sensibly.

Saints are first of all ways: they make for identification with religious
heroes or for concrete decisions. They galvanise more readily than moral
imperatives, or theories, or even demands. They act upon the feelings.
Their power to convince springs from their concrete value. This is why the
reading of the lives of the saints has been a valued exercise in the
Christian tradition. Priests used to read in their breviary the life of the
saint celebrated in the liturgy of the day. These lives were hackneyed,
carried little precise information, and contained lessons conformable to
models of holiness current among the people and favoured by authority.
The breviary was a simple method of presenting an army of religious
heroes and it invited the person reciting it to take his place amongst them
by identifying with the marvellous actions of his forebears. Following St
Francis is much more attractive than to allow oneself to be persuaded of
the need for poverty in order to discover the riches of the kingdom of
God.

Models are not only ways; they can often become obstacles. By
stereotyping holiness they overvalue the forms of the past and do not
encourage the innovatory force of the Gospel. Every member of a religious order has seen for himself how many people who were virtuous by
the standards of the constitutions of an order have in effect contributed to
its ruin. Pig-headedness about the maintenance of outdated rules and
about the reproduction of received models has often frustrated rather
than encouraged evangelical vitality, whether apostolic or contemplative.
We need only recall all the debate about priest-workers in France in 1954
and the objections made by Rome. Rome said that it would be impossible
to say the breviary in such circumstances, it feared that meditation might
become impossible; in short, it could not see how the life-style of a
priest-worker could fit into that of a priest of St Sulpice. It would have
been more valuable to ask what evangelical or apostolic reason there was
for breaking with a certain clerical style. There is nothing to show that the
way Church authorities in the West have become so tight about the
problem of celibacy is not in the same class. The argument in favour of
celibacy has become essentially an appeal to tradition, it is not being
reassessed in terms of the challenges of the present. In this way attachment to the past becomes an obstacle to finding new ways of ministry.
Once the model is given, we do not have to blaze new paths. Holiness
which ought to be something invented creatively out of stereotypes
remains subject to fashion.

This may seem to be scandalous, but is is perfectly comprehensible.

Stereotypes of holiness conform to the exigencies of group survival and identity. The Catholic Church alone possesses an official and rigourous system of canonisation and the experts in belonging to the kingdom of God remain in touch with the organisation of the Church and with the problems which this raises. The Catholic Church is a hierarchic society in which male celibate clerics hold power. These same clerics are charged with preaching the Gospel and with exercising surveillance over the doctrinal unanimity of Christians. Their interests, both in terms of the power they wield and the doctrine they watch, coincide with the interests of the Church: they ensure its survival. To question their government and their teaching, to raise doubts about the model of the Church which they promote and perpetuate by their work and their direction is to fail the Gospel.

This concern to value those in charge of the Church is the reason, it seems to me, why so many bishops and religious are beatified. There are, no doubt, as one of the articles in this number establishes, also good financial reasons for this promotion to supreme honour on the part of the leaders of the Church. But economic reasons are rooted in political ones: the survival and vitality of a hierarchic group would be jeopardised if the leaders were suspected of not working with all their might for the holy end of the group.

Almost the same goes for the almost entirely celibate population of official heaven: the explanation is to be found not in the kingdom of heaven but in the organisation of the Church. It goes without saying that a Church that is directed by celibate leaders, whether legal or spiritual, and that ceaselessly exalts celibacy for those who are responsible for the Church, should be in favour of its official effects in eternity.

In short, official heaven reflects the interests of the earthly Church. This should occasion reflection, but not scandal. It is a matter of reflection in so far as this kind of peopling of heaven shows what are the dominant forces in the earthly Church, their variability according to different epochs and in consequence the fact that they do not therefore determine absolutely the orthodox reinterpretation of the Gospel. It is possible that lapses of memory that occur in this process of officialisation of holiness stem from lapses of memory or from lacunae in the Gospel witness of the Church of any given epoch. The way it peoples heaven betrays the conception it has of its relationship to this world.

The range of problems raised by this issue is limited; it would be impertinent to pretend to say everything about holiness. It makes no claim to judge; that would be indecorous. It brings out into the open social or ideal factors that relativise the official forms of holiness and compels us to ponder yet once again the inimitable way of Jesus of Nazareth. Jesus opens up the kingdom of God by reaching out to those who have lost hope, he eats with outcasts and prostitutes, he scandalises the righteous, he disturbs the experts in the ways of God. Then let us take a look at the dominant iconography since the renaissance and the way it presents the heavenly places and their inhabitants. The only people we see there are civilised people grouped after the manner of this world. They enter heaven dressed for town. Hagiographers have been eager to make original or popular personalities conform. Despite these correspondences, the attractive power that the Gospel exerts on those without hope breaks out: it is no doubt no accident that one of the people closest to Jesus was also one of the most popular and one of the most disturbing in the Church: Francis of Assisi. In him something other than group interest comes to light, even in the legends: an energy that derives from the Spirit and that bursts open all the too human criteria of the official designation of entry into the kingdom. Once again it becomes a hope for those who are not heroes.

CHRISTIAN DUQUOC

Translated by John Maxwell

Part I

Articles

Josep Rovira Belloso

The Nature of
Holiness in
Jesus of Nazareth

1. AN IMPERTINENT QUESTION ON A SERIOUS TOPIC

IN A short span of time, I have seen the following surprising question asked in theological circles and, more indirectly, in a review for the clergy: Would Jesus of Nazareth be canonised today?

Taken literally, the question can quickly be dismissed as impertinent and even absurd. It is, of course, the holy figure of Jesus that establishes every criterion of holiness and not the other way round: no pre-established criterion can decide whether or not Jesus was a saint.

The virtue of this presumptuous question, however, is that it forces us to realise, in all its implications, that the supreme image and criterion of holiness are to be found only in the strange and intractable figure of Jesus of Nazareth—intractable in the sense that he cannot be encompassed in a set of formulae.

Furthermore, the question contains a critical burden worth taking seriously: it implicity prompts comparison between the 'wild genius'[1] of the holiness of Jesus and the more or less conventional models and criteria of holiness expressed in somewhat simplistic formulations such as, 'She was content to carry out her rule with the help of God's grace', or 'He accepted his sufferings with patience', etc. Seen in this light, the question whether Jesus would be canonised today takes on this new critical aspect: How is it that the holiness of the Messiah cannot be contained in any established mould of holiness, including that of several saints canonised in recent times who lack the anthropological—in rela-

3

tion to all men—and evangelical—in relation to believers and their followers—significance possessed by the holiness of the Master?

Our disturbing question finally enshrines one richer in theological content: What is the precise nature of the holiness of Jesus of Nazareth? This second question, with its radical questioning of certain recent canonisations, is much more closely related to the real history of Jesus. The problem is this: it was the just men—the 'saints'—of his time who condemned him, not the recognised sinners. This being so, we have to enquire deeply into the nature of a sanctity that so disconcerted those who took their religion seriously: the legitimate authorities of Judaism and the virtuous of their time.

Was it just the bigoted ill will of those who considered themselves just that inspired their total lack of understanding when faced with a disconcerting Jesus who broke into their religious world with his halo of Messianic pretensions, or was it something special in the holiness of Jesus that bore his power to disconcert as its own fruit?

So the real question is this: What specific characteristic of the holiness of Jesus not only broke the established canons of holiness in his own day—to the extent that his contemporaries were provoked to hostility and finally to condemning him—but still has the power to disconcert us today?

This is the serious topic underlying the impertinent question.

2. JESUS AND THE DISCONCERTMENT OF HIS CONTEMPORARIES

The sanctity of Jesus can be presented as a harmonic whole. But not as a harmony that excludes dissonant notes. On the contrary, as with Mozart's famous quartet, the holy life of Jesus functions as a higher harmony which integrates 'le disonanze'.

Or, to take an image from science, the sanctity of Jesus can be compared to the principles of relativity, in which the dimension of time-speed is added to the three spatial dimensions, affecting not only the object that moves but the whole continent surrounding it. This comparison tries to show that Jesus involves not only the full spread of human dimensions, but also an invasion by the transcendent or divine dimension, the fourth dimension constituting the secret of Jesus' existence, over which hovers the dynamic impulse of the all-embracing love of the Father. The element of disconcertment appears most strongly when this fourth dimension is seen to have a most unexpected relationship to human history.

This can be seen in action in the beginning of St Mark's gospel, whose first chapter is an emphatic account of the impact of the teaching and 'power' of the Messiah, followed (Mark 2:3-3:6) by five scenes showing truly disconcerting 'sayings' (logia) and actions on the part of Jesus. These are those where Jesus forgives the paralytic his sins, eats with sinners, approves those who do not fast while praising new wine in fresh skins, affirms his dominion over the sabbath, and finally 'breaks' the sabbath by curing the man with the withered hand.

To say that the disconcertment of Jesus' contemporaries stems from the fact that his words and actions are marked by paradox would not seem to reach the nub of the question; at least not without showing what the paradox consists of, not without revealing the content, paradoxical if one will, of the words and actions that disconcerted listeners and spectators. What, then, is this content?

If Jesus had limited himself to invoking God's forgiveness, instead of himself issuing the pardon, if he had praised tradition instead of novelty, if he had condemned sinners as ungrateful to God and avoided their company, eating only with the 'just' as an unmistakable sign that he was going to gather a community of the holy, if he had said there was nothing more holy than the sabbath because it was the day God rested and confined himself to its observance instead of showing himself its Lord in words and deeds—if he had done all these things, then he would not have overstepped the bounds of holiness as it was understood by strict Judaism, nor the limits of common sense.

Does the fact that he did none of these things show his aim to be a paradoxical contradiction of good religious observance, and a transgression of religious and legal rules with the presumption of a Faust or Prometheus? There is certainly '*para-dox*' (opinion contrary to the common). There is certainly transgression of 'legal devotion'. But I do not think this is yet the central character of the holiness of the Messiah.

3. THE DISCONCERTING ELEMENT IN THE SANCTITY OF JESUS

The essential, specific characteristic of Jesus' attitude as shown in these passages of the second gospel, and others similar, seems to me to consist—in the first place—in the fact that Christ, rather than carrying out some observance or pious act in order to please God, sets himself up as the centre of divine life and of God's salvation for men. And, in the second place, in the fact that these men are the sinners, the poor, those possessed by evil spirits, those who live on the fringes of society, those who, in a word, lack fulness in their lives.

(*a*) The fact that Christ sets himself up as an expansive centre of God's life and salvation supposes the incursion into this world of something that transcends it.

It supposes the incursion of the love of a forgiving God; it supposes that Jesus in the centre of a community that attracts, welcomes and collects sinners; it supposes him acting as the bridegroom bringing cheer to his guests at his wedding feast; it supposes that he is Lord of the sabbath and the source of salvation for the whole man.

This central characteristic of Jesus is best expressed, on a higher theological plane, in the well-known phrases of the 'I am' type, found above all in St John: I am forgiveness; I am the centre of the community of sinners; I am the bridegroom; I am the Lord of the sabbath; I am salvation and life. This makes it possible to speak of the arrival of the holiness of God himself in the midst of humanity. And it makes Jesus, rather than someone trying to carry out the law to the letter or establish religious observance as a supreme value, the man who in his person, words and actions, shows and expresses the gratuitous and saving love of God for those lacking fulness in their lives. This 'ontological' quality—of super-fulness—that characterises the holiness of Jesus, forms a first element of shock—the incursion of the divine in such a man—paradoxical and disconcerting in its effect: chapters six and eight of St John provide good evidence of this.

(b) This incursion of the divine is accompanied by a second disconcerting element, in that the power and fulness of Jesus are directed primarily to raising up the 'non-man',[2] brought about through the humiliation of Jesus the Christ.

The descending dynamic that leads to the 'humiliation of power' in Jesus is indeed disconcerting. He did not preach in Athens or in Rome, but 'by the lakeside'. In a land without prestige ('Galilee of the unbelievers') and without culture. He preached not from above, but from below, in solidarity with those who had no power, who did not count.

What is truly disconcerting about Jesus is not merely the irruption of the divine in his person, but his presence in the company of those who did not count. He did not place himself next to Caesar but alongside the victims of society. The upward movement of society is reflected in negative in Jesus, because he took the part of the hungry and the thirsty, the homeless, the sick and the prisoner. His final place on the social scale was that of a man condemned to death for the religious crime of blasphemy or the civil crime of sedition. 'Only those who have fallen from their estate and are being persecuted, the lost sentry, the buried soldier . . . the least free, are those who embody liberty', says Adorno.[3] Underlying these words one can hear the paradox expressed by St Paul: 'He made himself accursed to free us from the curse of the law'. Jesus appears simply as 'the last of men' and his words as 'last words', as of someone cut off from life.[4]

(c) The fact that Jesus acts from below, from the base of the humiliated and in the line of the liberation that stems from love (see Ps. 18:20), gives rise to the third disconcerting element, after the super-fulness and the humiliation: this is the element of transgression.[5]

Laws can be changed from above when they no longer fulfil the purpose for which they were promulgated. But what happens when a widening or sublimation of the purpose of the law is brought about from below? To the bystander, this is transgression of the established order.

Why was the sabbath apparently 'transgressed'?

Because, for Jesus, the law is certainly important, but still more so is the new finality of the law he himself established by setting himself up as the measure of the new man.

Laws can be described as an attempt to outline in general and abstract terms the requirements that stem from a reality deserving of respect.[6] Laws are a sort of objective approximation to this reality, and give a generic indication of what our response should be if we are to recognise, respect and bolster this reality. But laws cannot capture reality in all its richness, nor can they fully display the ultimate purposes of the law, nor provide a detailed image of the proper response demanded by this reality.

When Jesus, on the other hand, claims to be the Lord of the sabbath, he is pointing out the ultimate aim of the law. He is not enshrining either subjectivism or *anomia* (the absence of all laws), but stating that he himself is the final measure of man and therefore also the measure of the degree of observance required by the law of the sabbath. What matters is not for men to comply with the letter of the rest demanded on the sabbath, but for them to achieve the measure of the new creation represented by Jesus, the new man. So the law is important for Jesus, but the ultimate value is not its material observance; it is the specific salvation of persons.

The sabbath is 'transgressed' just for the sake of this ultimate value: the salvation of man from his sin, from his sickness or loneliness, hunger and thirst. It is transgression through 'overflowing', through the outpouring of the spirit of Jesus putting himself in the place of 'non-men'. It is not simply a legal transgression: this would explain the famous *logion* which the sixth century Beza-Cantabrigensis Codex added to Luke 6:5: 'The same day, seeing a man working on the sabbath, he said to him, "If you know what you are doing, you are blessed; but if you are doing it without knowing, you are a sinner and breaking the sabbath"'. Neither Promethean transgression nor irresponsibility are condoned in the sayings of Jesus.

What the invasion of Jesus by the love of the Father and the gift of the Spirit sealing or anointing the unfortunate on the Cross produce is this ontological fulness: this excess or overflow surpassing the legal and religious framework of his age and even of ours, which by creating a category of 'transgression through the divine overflowing the legal framework', shatters all yesterday and today's 'official' moulds of sanctity.

Let us now try to look at this in more particular historical detail.

4. THE DISCONCERTMENT PRODUCED BY JESUS TAKING ON HUMAN HISTORY AND STRUGGLING AGAINST THE EVILS AFFLICTING GROUPS OF INDIVIDUALS

Jesus' involvement in the world around him and the history of his time point the way to three formulations designed to grasp the specificity of the holiness of the Messiah. Basically, they say the same as the foregoing, but try to show it in relation to the real history of men, which Jesus shared.

1. The holiness of Jesus was applied to the real life of his day, not kept aside from its history.

It was precisely in this history that he opened a new way of justice, a new form of life leading to the Father through a positive relationship with people. That Jesus takes history upon himself is shown by the settings of Luke 3:1-2 and John 1:14. Jesus is the word of God living in a particular historical situation in which he adopts a position of one stripped of all attributes of wordly power.

Jesus did not shrink from the problems deriving from man's historicity, but faced them from the standpoint of his 'holy' freedom: he justified himself as a free man before Herod (Luke 13:32), tackling the most important political problem of his time, clarifying the relationship between the kingdom of God and the kingdom of the Roman Emperor: distinction, fusion or incompatibility? The passage concerning the tribute to Caesar (Matt. 22:21) should be read primarily in this sense: not as a treatise on constitutional law but as an illustration of the decision proper to the 'holy one of God', expressing his *holy* freedom.

Jesus possessed a 'sense of history', not in the sense of having a 'concept' or 'theory' of history, but in the sense that he could, first, take account of temporality as a dimension inherent in human existence ('The time will come . . .', he says in Mark 2:19 and Luke 17:22), and, above all, in the sense—though without attempting to elucidate the 'substance' of history or its 'motor', since he was not a St Augustine, nor a Hegel or Marx *avant la lettre*—of seeing clearly that human history could be lived as 'transcendence in history' or as history bordering on transcendence. This is most important, since in this light the gospel appears as the offering made to man so that he can meet God from the starting point of the facts of his own human existence, can develop his freedom on the basis of a particular situation, and can love with a true love that will find its object even in the most desperate situations. (Which, of course, is compatible with the earlier possibilities of relating to God through prayer and developing a liberated freedom.)

All this is possible because Jesus, the expression of the truth, love and freedom of God, has entered into our history and is the horizon of every possible human situation—all of which, through reference to him, take on fully human content and meaning.

2. The holiness of Jesus accepts the evil in history and, prophetically and actually, challenges the agents of evil in the world.

The holiness of Jesus unfolded not on the margins of the evil that enslaves all mankind, but in a strange militant and liberating antithesis passing through his sacrifice on the Cross.

A holiness that bore no relation to the evils that afflict mankind—in Upper Egypt, Naples or wherever—would be inconceivable, and this is why we react critically to formulations of sanctity of the 'She was content to carry out her rule with the help of God's grace' type. Any Christian saint, on a correct analysis of his or her life, will be seen to share with the Lamb of God the task of 'bearing and taking away' the sin of the world, since the sanctity of Jesus implies this element of response to the evil and suffering inherent in the world.

The first three chapters of Mark seek, deliberately, to give us the impression of the 'strength' of the love of God invading the world as a decisive episode in the struggle against evil. The demoniac element in man, sickness and ignorance, yield and withdraw when confronted by 'the holy one of God'.

Jesus is not concerned with praising man, nor with laying the foundations of an idealist anthropology seeking to define the 'essence' of man. This essence springs out and defines itself both from the man given over to this force of faithful love and from the man who receives the effects of this true and effective love. Jesus starts from the individual man, lacking as he is in various attributes that could contribute to his humanity, and, with God's love, re-makes this man starting with the very lack or deficiency that disfigures him.

This brings us to the third aspect:

3. Jesus takes on the particular situation of individuals, relates to them and in them creates the image of the new man, called to fulness, which consists in likeness to the image of the new man who Christ is.

There is here something very central to the holiness of Jesus, which I would call the 'capacity to reach men'. Jesus flees from any ideologisation: he does not seek to build a system based on principles and leading to conclusions perhaps believed by human experience. He realises that he can reach men's hearts with his words (see John 2:25) and through his actions—actions that bring the kingdom of God amongst us[7]—he reaches situations where men lack bread (the scene in the desert), or enlightenment (Nicodemus or the woman taken in adultery), conversion (Zaccheus), mission and meaning in their lives (the Apostles), personality (those possessed by evil spirits), liberty (the Pharisees), giving all a new meaning in their lives, changing the situation of those individuals.[8]

Where ideology is a maze, the gospel is a short-cut to the centre of man, bringing him salvation as a new content of and horizon to life. If there is an element of transgression in this, something not sought in itself but simply an effect of the excess of divinity and its divine freedom in Jesus, there is now another category characterising the sanctity of Jesus: the 'break' produced by his struggle against evil and his attitude—defenceless but unequivocal—to its agents in the world.

Jesus stands in contrast to the inertia of the world and, not from personal animosity but by virtue of the dynamics of faith, brings about a break with Phariseeism, with the religiosity of his day and with the established powers that were to bring him to the Cross. The Cross itself is the archetypal break with the 'ways of the world', and synthesises all the disconcerting elements apparent in the sanctity of the Messiah.

5. SYNTHESIS: THE CROSS

In effect, the synthesis of the threefold disconcertment produced by Jesus is summed up and heightened by something greater than the out-pouring of divinity, the humiliation and the transgression that lead to definite breaks with the world and its powers. This is the *scandal* of the Cross. 'Happy is the man who does not lose faith in me', Jesus exclaims after evoking the liberating approach of the Messiah as foretold in Isaiah (Matt 11:6; Luke 7:23). In the Cross there is, clearly, the humiliation of the Lord, and, equally, the consequence of Jesus' break with the estab-lished powers and the letter of the law; these we can *see,* but we can only *keep faith in* and *love* the invasion of the divine at this moment of supreme contradiction and powerlessness.

To see the Cross only as a state of suffering, however, would be inconsistent with what we have seen of the relationship between the sanctity of Jesus and history. It is a historical idealism purely to equate the Cross with suffering. The Cross is suffering placed by 'the world and the flesh' on the shoulders of the just man who shared the lowest place with 'non-men' in order to bring them out of this lowest place (see *Gaudium et Spes* 38a). It is the suffering of the just man Jesus *as he shares in* the fate of the hapless, for which he was taken outside the city walls, without honour and without decorum, set aside as a man condemned to death.

This, in itself, is scandalous. The scandal, however, becomes a mystery, and a mystery of happiness, when we *believe* that the will of the Father was brought about on the Cross. It was necessary for the Messiah to suffer—sharing the poverty of the poor so as to enrich them with his life (see 2 Cor. 8:9)—and so enter into his glory! Only by treading this path could he finally share this glory with all the sufferers in the world.

So, in the end, the holiness of Jesus becomes the mystery of the blessing of God the Father on the Christ on the Cross and the 'opening up' of a new and fruitful way for man to recover his freedom, his human dignity and his destiny as son of God.

The Cross is the synthesis of the holiness of Jesus because it is the most radical embodiment of the lowest place taken by 'the Holy and Just', by the 'Author of Life' (Acts 3:14-15); it is the ultimate expression of the vengeance wreaked by the transgressed law on the just man. But it also sums up the holiness of Jesus in that his 'last words' on the Cross suggest the welcome and response of life with which the Father responds to the faithful love, submissive to the end, of his chosen Son. Happy is the man who does not lose faith and accepts as God's salvation the fact that Jesus—precisely because he is God's anointed, the Son of God—neither wished to nor 'could' come down from this place of obedience to the Father and to men. Jesus, at once generous and dutiful, made himself obedient to the will of the Father not only in prayer but also on the Cross. In prayer, he saw the will of the Father as an all-embracing desire for life allowing no-one to be lost (see John 6:39) but willing all to have abundant life through a personal gift of true and faithful love (see John 10:10 and 1:14, 17b). On the Cross, Jesus accepted the paradoxical working-out—without power or glory—of this will whose divine nature enabled it to be worked out in total defencelessness, with none of the trappings of worldly power.[9]

Jesus—and all mankind with him—did not merely passively accept the will of God but brought it to fruition actively, freely and responsibly through the scandal of the Cross, through an unmeasured submission. His actions (*poiein*) on the Cross were as defenceless as God himself; he showed his divinity, in the most disconcerting way on the Cross, in the fact that he never used the 'powers' of the world in his mission and rejected any temptation to use them. Love alone shines out from the Cross of Christ, in all its 'powerless strength': in the life-giving response of the Father and in the gift of the Spirit of the Risen Christ to men, since this gift is our foretaste of God's response of final salvation which is the resurrection, which has already begun in the life of faith.

This is not to reduce the resurrection to the Cross; it is to recognise, with 'believing incredulity', that the humiliation of the Son is the only starting point from which humanity can be raised to live on the 'farther shore' of the Father. On the way to this shore, only the love that sets us free (Ps. 18:20) is worthy of faith.

6. FINAL NOTE: PASTORAL CONSEQUENCES

The paradigmatic nature of the holiness of Jesus for the Church and for Christians implies a whole host of pastoral consequences to be derived from consideration of it. But there is one central one: Jesus' Institution cannot be the institutionalisation of accepted norms, not even of religious norms. It cannot present sanctity or the Christian life as simply fulfilling a rule established *a priori,* without taking account of the struggle against the evil afflicting mankind, or of the history, with its lights and darks, in which mankind moves. The holiness of the Christian has to move through this history along the conductor rail of transcendence, signalled by the passage of God through it.

This central idea can be broken down into three statements:

(*a*) The Institution of Jesus is none other than the institution of the Spirit, poured out without measure from the superabundance of the Cross. What Christ instituted through his Messianic fulness, that is with the gift of the Spirit, is the *Ecclesia orans.*

(*b*) The Institution of Jesus cannot share the place of Caesar or the highest places in the empires of any period. The perennial temptation of Constaninism consists in trying to drag the Church up from the lowest place, out of the company of the simple and the deprived whom it should accompany till they are made into the new man created in Christ Jesus. What Jesus instituted through his humiliation is that Church which we pray in Canon II will 'come to perfection in love'.

(*c*) The Institution of Jesus is not only one of a critical consciousness in society, but of prophecy—in action—of freedom for those who do not possess it. It finds its true identity in the meeting of and relationship with 'non-men' whom it restores 'healed' to the presence of God and their brothers. The Church instituted by Jesus, a man freely obedient to the Father, is the sacrament of man's salvation. God's decisive action, mediated in the world by the Church as instrument of the kingdom, flagrantly subverts, 'transgresses', the ways of the world and its weight of oppression, division and death, in order to bring about communion between God and man and among men.

Translated by Paul Burns

Notes

1. See *Correspondència de Diàleg Eclesial* 176 (Feb. 1979) 4.

2. This phrase, first used by Leonard Boff, and developed by the Catalan novelist Manuel de Pedrodo, designated what Robert Musil was to call 'the man without qualities'.

3. T. W. Adorno *Mahler* (Paris 1976) p. 244.

4. In my article 'Jesucristo único y universal' in *Jesucristo en la Historia y en la Fe* (Madrid 1977) pp. 303-315, I tried to show that there are two very significant ways of looking at Jesus: as the Word of God and as the 'last among men'.

5. C. Duquoc has studied this element of 'transgression that liberates' in *Dieu différent* (Paris 1977) pp. 43-60, in 'El Dios de Jesus y la crisis de Dios en nuestro tiempo', and in the work cited in the previous note, pp. 39-50.

6. E. Schillebeeckx *Dieu et l'homme* (Brussels 1965) p. 233 ff.

7. R. Schnackenburg *Gottes Herrschaft und Reich* (Freiburg[4] 1965); *id. El evangelio de San Marcos* (Barcelona 1972) p. 38.

8. Jesus personalises and makes people act as persons: see J. Rovira 'Una promesa de vida' in *La set de viure* (Barcelona 1979) p. 32.

9. J. González-Faus *El Acceso a Jesus* (Salamanca 1979) p. 268.

Pierre Delooz

The Social Function
of the
Canonisation of Saints

IN A collection of studies devoted to spirituality the theme of canonisation calls for explanation; even in a symposium on sanctity it would require some comment. For although the link between canonisation and sanctity may seem self-evident, it will be useful to examine it for that very reason.

It is not possible to consider this connection closely in a few pages, across the two thousand years of the Church's history. The most one can do is to indicate some of the questions that arise. These prove interesting.

But, first of all, we must define canonisation. It is the decision to grant someone a public and mandatory cult, a decision duly proclaimed by the competent Church authority. Clearly this definition does not refer to sanctity in direct terms. It emerges, however, by implication, during the juridical process which the authority employs in so far as this public cult is only granted to individuals whose sanctity is recognised as wholly acceptable by the authority itself. If we take this definition as a starting-point we may find ourselves asking a series of questions. Who is the competent authority? What does it mean by a mandatory, public cult? What kind of sanctity is wholly acceptable? The answers are not straightforward. As we have noted, two thousand years of history should be taken into account, in churches established in vastly different settings. Consider an illustration. In the cultural milieu of the Graeco-Roman period, picture a bishop at work in some small country town in a distant corner of the Empire. As he took ceremonial steps to elevate the relics of a martyr he was unquestionably the agent of canonisation. But his procedure would

certainly not be exactly the same, detail by detail, as the action of Pope
Pius XII as he canonised Pope Pius X. It is not only that the competent
authority is no longer the same, the concept of a mandatory public cult
has changed and the qualifications necessary for sanctity have developed
over the years. It would probably have been extremely difficult for a
bishop of the Roman Empire to picture himself as not being the competent authority, or to imagine that a time would come when a distinction
would be drawn between a permitted and a mandatory public cult; or,
indeed, to conceive it possible to venerate a person who had died peace-
fully in his bed. One of the reasons for such change lies precisely in the
fact that the social role of canonisation has altered. In view of the purpose
of this article we shall concentrate on particular aspects of this question;
we appreciate that other points could be raised.

If we approach canonisation from the standpoint of its social role, the
question at once arises of what use it is being put to, in other words of the
functions that it fulfils. It is common knowledge that such functions can be
either obvious to the eye or—in varying degrees—obscure, hidden from
the people involved. But who are these people? To whom is canonisation
useful? Certainly not to the person who has been canonised. That only
happens to dead people. There is already plenty of material here for
comment, but we must proceed. In any case canonisation serves to
reinforce the authority of the one who canonises. There is no need, at this
juncture, to stress the significance of the progressive shift from episcopal
to papal canonisation. This movement did not occur smoothly. When the
bishops met in Council at the Lateran in AD 993 under the presidency of
John XV they hardly realised what they were doing. In associating the
pope with the canonisation of Ulric of Augsburg they were helping to
divest themselves of a right they had possessed for a thousand years. That
is certainly what happened. The right of canonisation was reserved to the
pope by the early codification of Canon Law known as The Decretals of
Gregory IX and issued in 1234. At first it is doubtful whether the bishops
paid a great deal of attention to this monopoly. It was not until the
time of Urban VIII in 1634 that this papal prerogative was—almost
universally—recognised.

In a short study like the present one it is again out of the question to
describe the numerous gambits that emerged during the extremely long
period of episcopal canonisations or the many variants of collegiality that
were used for the purpose. We shall be confining ourselves to canonisations by the popes. The function of these has clearly been to strengthen
papal authority. In fact they represent part of Rome's over-all secular
strategy of reinforcing the hierarchical centre of the Church. Between the
time of Gregory VII and the present this process has, of course, taken
innumerable forms. Nevertheless papal canonisation was rarely aimed at

a direct and unequivocal assertion of the pope's authority. It was exceptional when Alexander III canonised Thomas Becket in a clash with the King of England; similarly when Benedict XIII canonised Gregory VII it was to let the leaders of the Enlightenment know how his mind worked. They understood the message admirably. In general, papal canonisation had a double aim: negatively it sought to prevent bishops from deciding by themselves who could be publicly venerated; and more positively and particularly, its aim was to monitor and control popular piety.

We have already raised the first part of the question; now we must turn our gaze to that collective actor on the stage of life—the Christian community. It has always been a fact that the process of canonisation has taken its origin among the ordinary believers rather than the holders of power. If anyone is going to be made a saint, that person must have already been discerned as holy by some part of the people of God. This social discernment is quite fundamental. Without it the authorities will undertake nothing. But this popular recognition is not enough in itself. It must be matched by a pressure exerted on the authority which will associate it with the cult that has arisen so naturally. In this way the cult will gain the status of a public cult, an official process, done in the Church's name. For fifteen centuries first the bishops, and later the pope, have been led by God's people to confirm an initiative that the people themselves have made. This was exactly what canonisation was. A social perception is confirmed as a result of social pressure. It is still like that, but there is a considerable difference. Ever since the time of Urban VIII the cult has been allowed only after canonisation, whereas before that it had to have been in existence already. Thus what had been indispensable (namely a cult already in existence) is now forbidden; in fact, its existence could itself represent grounds for refusing canonisation. There is no need to emphasise once more the increase of papal intervention in the matter. Since the seventeenth century the authority has no longer been satisfied with confirming a perception felt locally and expressed in a cult. The cult can only be observed if the authority has explicitly so decided. There is no question of allowing any anticipation or presumption of such a decision.

This monitoring of popular devotion is of interest for more reasons than one. Let us pause to consider the juridical tests created to ensure the sanctity of a person who has been nominated as a result of social perception and pressure. These tests have been progressively relaxed.

(a) The test that goes furthest back and is the most traditional is martyrdom. This special cult of the dead, focusing on the martyrs, arose as a direct result of believers dying for Christ at the violent hands of persecutors. This criterion is not as straightforward as at first appears. There is the need to decide what is a genuine martyrdom and what is not. For instance, a heretic cannot die for Christ. As learned a man as Pope

Benedict XIV could hold the view, in the eighteenth centry, that a pseudo-martyrdom of this kind was an indication of the devil's power over the human heart. The genuine martyr lays down his life not only for Christ but also for his true Church: or, at least, within the framework of her life. Once more we see the authority keeping a careful eye on who may be safely venerated as a saint without endangering the authority itself. Besides, a decision as to what is or is not a religious context that would fittingly lead to martyrdom also depends on the way the religious authority at any given moment sees things. Speaking very generally, it can be said that the infliction of violent death that constitutes martyrdom is decided partly on political grounds. Nowadays the papal authority holds the prerogative in weighing up the relative importance of religious and political dimensions. Changing situations in this area of thought and action have surely led to changes in decision-making. Could one unhesitatingly declare today that Pierre Arbuès would be canonised: an inquisitor killed by the comrades of his victims? In China in the course of the Boxer Rising hundreds of foreigners and Christians were killed in a wave of xenophobic antipathy. Who were martyrs among that multitude? Not the Protestants perhaps, but even among the Catholics? Was Maria Goretti a martyr? She was killed by a young man whose sexual advances she had repulsed. 'Yes', replied Pius XII, 'she was a martyr'. In this way he wanted to reinforce moral teaching. People are always martyrs to those who recognise them! That is why it is necessary to check such recognition, for popular devotion could be wrongly motivated.

(*b*) Without disappearing altogether, martyrdom was increasingly replaced by another criterion of choice: a heroic quality of virtue. This was clearly a relative concept, and the Christian community could not be allowed to be sole judge of it. At any given moment in history everything turns on how far the ecclesiastical authority is prepared to go in treating as virtuous anything above the average. Guided though it is by legal precedents and procedures, this evaluation inevitably gives way to practical considerations, of pastoral or other kinds. Social roles and pressures come into play, and ultimately these are judged solely by those who wield authority. At this juncture the concept of a model to be followed suggests itself. But in practice this is hardly used explicitly at all. For example the Catechism of Peter Canisius is typical of the whole tradition when it describes the saints as primarily one who intercedes before God. Any suggestion that the saint might be imitated is purely incidental. Besides any imitation that is mentioned is quite different in kind from anything covered by the modern concept of a model. The saint is to be copied because he lets God act. The *Acta Sanctorum* are *gesta Dei per sanctos*. We shall be coming back to this question.

(*c*) There is another criterion that has emerged explicitly since the seventeenth century and is part of the process of canonisation. I refer to the writings and their orthodoxy. One might easily think that this is an area where the authorities operate with a royal freedom. And yet this matter of orthodoxy always involves relative judgements, for it depends on the convictions held by the one who decides. So it was that Robert Bellarmine was placed on the Index by Sextus V, but was later canonised by Pius XI and proclaimed as a doctor of the Church. In between the two decisions the doctrinal position of the popes had changed, and thus writings that had been rejected became praise-worthy.

(*d*) The last test, still to be observed, is miracle. This subject deserves a study in depth, but barely an outline can be offered here. Meanwhile, however, we can say that for a long time miracle was deemed decisive, and yet its importance is apparently waning: indeed, in some instances, has even disappeared. Thus Gregory Barbarigo was canonised by John XXIII without a miracle. This represents a major departure from the practice of the Middle Ages. During that period being a saint meant doing miracles on a large scale. And miracles were also *gesta Dei per sanctos*. It is true that the papal power reserved to itself the right to assess these miracles. After all, rebels like Simon de Montfort had palpably done miracles by the dozen; and everyone knows that the devil himself is adept at them and uses them to trick the human race. So it has come about that miracles too are subject to the scrutiny of the papal hierarchy. They are indeed the product of popular devotion and the the confident petition of ordinary believers, but the decisions are made at the top. Experience suggests that those in control are becoming increasingly awkward in the matter. Is this the reason why ordinary believers get fewer and fewer miracles? Time was when miracles were put forward, in connection with a cause for canonisation, by the score, or indeed by the hundred. Today people find it quite hard to produce the two that are obligatory. In fact when the wish was expressed for John Ogilvie to be canonised, Rome herself indicated that she would be satisfied by a single miracle. As I see it, a kind of negotiating process seems to exist between the Roman curia and the postulators, which produces the exact number of miracles that have to be supplied. In group canonisation it is the normal practice. Thus it was on the basis of two miracles attributed to the group that the Forty Martyrs in England were canonised. It is by this device too that the monitoring function of the central power is clearly seen. Further it is becoming evident that the nature of miracles themselves has changed. The old diversity has narrowed down to isolated cures that cannot be explained by medicine. A certain number of doctors are called in to give an opinion, but the papal authority is the final arbiter. At the same time, although the pope is in this way well-equipped with criteria that depend in the end on his powers of discretion, he cannot make saints as he pleases. As we have already remarked, there must first come a movement, a perception, a pressure from the grass roots.

To survey this territory would yield some interesting results, but we must content ourselves with a comment regarding the specific papal power that needs to be convinced; it is not the pope himself but the organisation of the curia that has canonisations within its competence. (Historically this has been the Congregation of Rites, but since 1969 it has been the Congregation for the Causes of Saints.) This is not a trivial point that we are making. There is a whole world of difference between John XV's action already described when he gave approval to a cult rendered to a saint after listening in Council to the details of his life, and the highly-stylised proceedings of a permanent bureaucracy. This vast change can be remarked in many ways; one of them appears clearly if we observe the role of the ordinary believers at ground level. For more than a thousand years their role was direct and decisive. It was the Christian community which venerated a tomb and obtained miracles. The ecclesiastical machine barely intruded. It only acted when necessary in order to avoid any possible abuses of procedure or to quell them and also to take responsibility for precedents already established. The process of bureaucratisation—using that term in its most positive sense—was bound to affect canonisation by reducing sharply the popular character of the selection of saints. Nowadays it falls to specialist civil servants to check in detail the data provided by local insight. Such data will be duly submitted to rules which are inevitably impersonal, and criteria will be applied that are essentially juridical. What this procedure gains in thoroughness, it quickly loses in ponderous and expensive delays. Indeed for some centuries now it has no longer been possible to envisage a canonisation without an accompanying pressure-group, having at its own disposal a supply of specialists, time and capital. It has been found in practice that the ideal lobby turns out to be the religious congregation. It has the resources to obtain the services of a good postulator; it can face the risk of a prolonged process needing great perseverance: proceedings have been known to last for more than a century; a religious congregation is able to lay its hands on the sums needed in one way or another to cover a process that is painstakingly careful. It is almost impossible for any layman to be able to meet these conditions. What he must do is to find a religious congregation that would think it rewarding to take over his case. This happened for example with the Uganda Martyrs who had been shining lights of one of the missions of the White Fathers. Conversely it is easy to understand the special chance of success of a cause advancing the founding figure of a religious congregation. Such a man or woman possesses the ideal conditions for advancement.

The channels of bureaucracy have made it so difficult for a lay person to be canonised that the perception of sanctity has itself been affected. The waiting-lists published by the Congregation concerned confirm this. Priests and particularly the men and women who founded religious congregations represent an overwhelming majority, even before the bureaucratic investigation of their cause begins. To use the jargon of the day, we have here a typically ideological phenomenon, in so far as the authority is capable of so directing the attention of the faithful that it ensures the official conception of social cohesion and at the same time legitimates the authority's own position. The one who is canonised is not any servant of God you care to name, but the person whom the authority in Rome has, by previous definition, declared acceptable. It practically inhibits all perception that fails to conform. There is really nothing astonishing about all this. All authority in high places inevitably acts in this way. As we have already said, however, the hold of the authority on social perception is not total. There are particular changes that operate in the social structure of the Church which inescapably modify the perception of the faithful, and, as a consequence, alter in due course the practice and teaching of the authority itself. We shall give some examples.

For nearly ten centuries it was the papal tradition very frequently to canonise men and, only rarely, women. Between the tenth and nineteenth centuries Rome canonised 87 per cent men and only 13 per cent women. This obviously reflects a pattern that heavily favours the males and that corresponds predictably with the traditionally inferior view of women in the Church. The twentieth century shows a difference. The proportion becomes 75 per cent of men to 25 per cent of women. This has happened without any change in the procedure that would favour women. What has really occurred is that a change has taken place in social perception and social pressure, and this has produced attitudes that have increased women's status in the Church; they are, however, still treated as a minority. Thus there are changes in social perception which correspond to the changes in social structure, and the Church establishment has in no way been their cause. Beatifications—a first step towards canonisation since the seventeenth century—have produced the same results. Table I allows this trend to be set out in statistical detail.

In another field a similar shift in the social structures has affected the social perception of sanctity, but not to the same extent. I am referring to the relationship between the clergy and the laity. If we define the word 'clerical' as signifying generally anything that is not considered to be lay, it can be stated baldly that the Catholic Church has been controlled by clerical forces during the period covered by our study. This is manifestly true, and is illustrated perfectly by the way in which canonisations work. We have already indicated that the procedure has favoured clergy of all kinds. For they had at their disposal the pressure-group needed to let

Table I

(showing Canonisations and Beatifications according to the period of their promulgation and the sex of the person promoted)

	Canonisations							Beatifications					
	Men		Women		Total		Men		Women		Total	
	No.	%	No.	%	No.	%	No.	%	No.	%	No.	%
10th-16th century	101	89	12	11	113	100						
17th-19th century	123	85	21	15	144	100	371	90	42	10	413	100
20th century[1]	127	75	42	25	169	100	629	74	218	26	847	100
Total	351	82	75	18	426	100	1000	79	260	21	1260	100

[1] Extending to the end of Paul VI's reign.

their cause succeed. Without any change in this procedure the percentage today of the laity among the saints can be seen to be slightly higher. The reason is that ecclesiastical lobbies have sponsored them. The majority of such lay people are martyrs, whose group-cause has been promoted through the endeavours of missionary congregations. Quite legitimately these have longed to see the glory of the fathers enhanced by the glory of their sons and daughters. Table II gives some indication of this phenomenon.

Table II

(showing Canonisations and Beatifications according to the period of their promulgation and the ecclesiastical status of the persons promoted)

	Canonisations							Beatifications					
	Clergy		Laity		Total		Clergy		Laity		Total	
	No.	%	No.	%	No.	%	No.	%	No.	%	No.	%
10th-16th century	88	82	19	18	107	100						
17th-19th century	111	81	26	19	137	100	197	60	134	40	331	100
20th century[2]	133	79	36	21	169	100	621	67	307	33	928	100
Total	332	81	81	19	413	100	818	65	441	35	1259	100

[2] These totals are smaller than in **Table I** because the ecclesiastical status of some of them is not known.

A fact which does not emerge clearly from Table II is the paucity of married lay saints. The category is scarcely represented at all. There are certainly some married people among those lay men and women beatified through the efforts of missionary congregations, but their number is small. Furthermore, their status (i.e., whether they are married or not) does not always arise during the procedures; this is surely significant. In any case, in many instances it is not possible to make a judgement.

There are also some married lay people among those who have been canonised. Thomas More is an example. Indeed he was married twice. But the married status of such saints has been quite incidental. Overall there is really only one instance where marriage has had to be taken into account seriously, and even then by a judicious stress on maternity: that of Anne-Marie Taïgi. She had the good fortune to be a tertiary of the Trinitarian order. The Trinitarians managed to advance her to beatification. Even today it would appear that those looking for sanctity find it hard to consider seriously the conjugal virtues. Celibacy, whether of those who have taken vows or not, is by far the most regular source of those who are canonised.

This leads us to pause once more over the concept of 'a model'. It would be necessary to consider very carefully before asserting that the canonised saint is a model. In what sense? In what way? Celibacy has been given special prominence century after century. The last layman (G. Moscati) to be beatified by Paul VI was a celibate. This prominence cannot be explained simply by the very great difficulty experienced under the present procedure by anyone seeking to promote the cause of persons who were not celibate, namely, the difficulty of finding an appropriate pressure-group. This difficulty is significant in itself. What the papal authority has proceeded to set forth as a model is certainly not the Christian life of a layman, living with his wife and family in the ordinary way. If this does cause difficulties today, it is probably because the view of sanctity held by our contemporaries has changed. But is there a problem here? One must know for sure, if there is. But the answer is far from clear. Consider the waiting lists to which we have already referred. They are issued by the Congregation for the Causes of Saints, under the title, *Index ac status causarum Beatificationis Servorum Dei et Canonizationis Beatorum*. The latest edition is 1975. In every case the waiting lists show that the canonisations in the making will share the same character with those of the past. Those who are awaiting official elevation are, for the most part, celibates. Would this be so, if social perception had fundamentally changed? There is only one point in the actual process at which any such change in social perception and pressure could be seen, and that would take place if permission were obtained from the appropriate department for one cause to be given priority over another. In this way the procedure would be expedited in favour of lay people and married lay people in particular. Only the future will tell whether this will take place. The proposals to this effect made at the last Council by Cardinal Suenens have not met with significant response. This is not due to reluctance on the part of the officials involved. They only give one cause priority over another if the pressure to do so is one they can accept. The postulator must have many qualities. Cleverness and the right background are not enough. Other gifts are essential. He should be able to supply every detail of information asked for without the slightest hesitation, and to give swift and satisfactory replies to any objections that may be raised. He should be able to put forward miracles that stand up to medical scrutiny and demonstrate the clear presence of the *fama sanctitatis* which we have so often recalled in our references to social perception and social pressure. Clearly the postulator is in no position to respond to these requirements of the bureaucracy unless some part of the Church has been deeply stirred to act—to provide the close attention, the enthusiasm and the money that are required so much. All this does not preclude the possibility of high-placed ecclesiastical dignitaries and the pope in particular from examining one dossier before another. This has happened, but the position in general has remained unchanged. It is exceptional for a pope to act in the manner of Clement X. In order to please his former fellow-diocesans of Camerino, he proceeded to canonise their old local hero, Venantius: leaving the responsibility of knowing exactly who he might really be to the historians of the future.

Nevertheless particular causes can capture the official attention, causes that reflect some special pastoral or political concern of the moment. In that case they win a priority that thereafter becomes the norm. In this way by canonising some Africans a stance was taken, designed to remove any suspicion of racism. One might even indulge in predictions. For instance there is a dossier in the files concerning Gianna Molla Beretta, mother of a family. She died seven days after bearing her fourth child. Now it seems that she had refused an abortion when there was probably still time to save her life. As she had a brother who was a Capuchin, the Capuchins have undertaken to promote her cause. In this way the necessary pressure-group is freely available. One could well imagine that a pope might interest himself in this cause in the context of a political gesture of censure against abortion. In any case the curia will certainly continue to verify details most carefully. In the nature of things it is reluctant to surrender its own power. It is equally true at the end of the day that perception and pressure from the grass roots must follow; otherwise the cause could fall under the heading of the Silent File— if we may make use of the *stylus curiae.*

Canonisation emerges, then, as an activity taking place at the confluence of two powerful rivers. One flows from God's people and the other from the various ecclesiastical authorities. That the second is stronger than the first is beyond question. There is a special reason for this which we have emphasised. The Church authorities are in a position to give strong guidance to the people of God when it makes choices. This is seen particularly in the influence they wield—ideological in character— on the world of ideas. The effect of Vatican II's thrust remains to be seen.

Will the centre be led to yield more autonomy to the circumference in this matter? The reasons would have to be very strong, for it would mean that the authority would be voluntarily divesting itself of a prerogative that took centuries to win. It would need nothing short of a different model of power. If this new model of power appeared, it would bring with it, I suspect, a different model of a saint.

Translated by Tom Baird

Bernard Plongeron

Concerning Mother Agnes of Jesus: Theme and Variations in Hagiography (1665-1963)

WITHOUT TWO unsuccessful moves for her beatification, in 1749 and 1808, Agnes Galand, a Dominican nun of the convent of St Catherine at Langeac in the diocese of Le Puy, would perhaps not have enjoyed the hagiographic fortune which, stretching as it does over three centuries, makes her an exemplary case for the historian.

There are three main reasons. First, Mother Agnes is claimed by two religious families with different spiritualities, the Order of Preachers and the Society of St Sulpice. A Dominican saint or a Sulpician saint? The ambivalence of this double attachment affects the construction of the model of Agnes' sanctity, and all the more since a third religious family, the Society of Jesus, also marked her in spiritual direction.

Already composite at its origin, the *vita* of Agnes of Jesus was constantly retouched over the centuries. This is a second reason for interest on the part of historians of spirituality and religious attitudes. The aim, from the seventeenth century to the present, has been to bring the cause of the Servant of God to a successful conclusion and, to this end, to modify her hagiography according to criteria capable of arousing popular fervour and winning conviction from the Roman judges. An excellent opportunity to measure the interlocking of the model of sanctity with contemporary culture.

Finally, having been restarted so often, the steps to promote the cause

25

in Rome have given rise to a wealth of archives which have been preserved at St Sulpice, notably for the cause of 1808. These documents
reveal unexpected aspects of the behind the scenes activity in a process
before the Congregation of Rites, at the beginning of the nineteenth
century and provide an initial contribution to a history of canonisations
which remains to be written and about which there remain many
obscurities.

1. MOTHER AGNES OF JESUS (1602-1634): HER LIFE AND THE FIRST HAGIOGRAPHIC CONSTRUCTION

Like most of the fifteen biographers who have been studying Mother
Agnes for three centuries,[1] we shall summarise her life without, for the
moment, considering the prodigies and miracles attached to it.

Agnes Galand was born at Puy-en-Velay on 17 November 1602 in a
petit bourgeois family; her father was a master cutler. Her religious
education was entrusted to the Jesuits at the college in Le Puy. She is
described as an adolescent with a marked bent for meditation, formed in a
Christocentric piety and a strong Marian devotion.

Frustrated by her father in her religious vocation, she remained in
society but in 1621 obtained from her new Dominican directors the habit
of the Third Order of St Dominic and took a secret vow of virginity. Her
tribulations increased: problems of health, spiritual torments (of a dia-
bolical nature) and the mocking incomprehension of her acquaintances
when she announced her wish to join in the establishment of the convent
for enclosed religious at Langeac.

Accepted at first as a lay sister—because of her humble origins, which
she was later to recall frequently—she became a choir sister. Shortly after
her solemn profession, in 1630, she was elected prioress. Jealousies and
administrative obstruction resulted in the annulment of this election.
Fourteen months later, Mother Agnes became novice-mistress, sub-
prioress and finally prioress.

It was at this period that there took place an extraordinary incident
which was later recorded and investigated in the process for beatification.
Jean-Jacques Olier (1608-1657), a worldly young priest, was completing
his priestly conversion under the direction of Vincent de Paul at Saint-
Lazare. During his retreat in March 1631 there appeared to him a woman
holding a crucifix in one hand and a rosary in the other. She told him that
she was praying for his conversion. The apparition took place a second
time. M. Olier thought at first that it was a vision of the Blessed Virgin,
but then realised that 'this wonderful apparition must be some religious
living in the world, and spared no effort to make careful investigations to

discover in what monastery she resided'. On her side, Mother Agnes, three years earlier, had been weeping during her prayers for the sins which were being committed in the world and in Auvergne in particular. She had a vision. 'Pray to my Son', she was told, 'for the abbé of Pébrac'. She was unaware that the abbey of Pébrac, fourteen kilometres south of Langeac, was in the charge of J.-J. Olier. Olier, who had undertaken the evangelisation of the Velay, had heard of the celebrated sanctity of a nun. The meeting took place at Langeac when Mother Agnes was ill and in the infirmary. 'I have seen you elsewhere, Mother', exclaimed the abbé of Pébrac. Agnes confirmed that she had appeared to him twice in Paris and revealed to him that he was destined to found seminaries in France. This was the beginning of the Society of Saint Sulpice, which Mother Agnes encouraged and supported during several further meetings with the founder, M. Olier.

Their spiritual union remained so close that, when Mother Agnes died on 19 October 1634 after a painful illness, M. Olier was mysteriously informed. The official news did not reach him until All Saints' Day while he was in the confessional, and he had difficulty in containing his emotion. In 1655 he personally supervised the removal of the body into a new coffin, more fitting than the old one, pending the final transfer, in 1841, to the monastery of Langeac, which had by then been rebuilt after the Revolution. Thereafter the faithful could venerate her in a coffin donated by the Viscountess D'Ussel, Agnes' biographer, and covered by a shrine of carved wood presented by the Sulpicians of Canada.

It was in 1698 that the process of beatification of the Dominican mystic had been opened, but in fact, through her, it was mysticism (theology and spirituality) which were under investigation. The basis was a *Life of the Venerable Mother Agnes of Jesus by an ordinary priest*, which remained the *mater lectionis* of all the hagiographic variations which were to follow.

This 'ordinary priest', who initially remained anonymous out of modesty, was M. de Lantages, the superior of the Sulpician seminary at Le Puy. Less than twenty years after Agnes' death he began to collect the main documents: a *Life of Sister Agnes Galand* (in manuscript) composed by Fr Esprit Panassière, O.P., the spiritual director of the religious, a long (anonymous) memoir by Fr Boyer, S.J., another of Agnes' directors direct testimonies collected in the region of Le Puy, where Agnes was known as 'the mother of the poor', and the reminiscences of Agnes' childhood and youth written by a former schoolfriend, herself the daughter of a merchant of Le Puy and later a Dominican nun at Viviers, Gabrielle Jacques, and finally an *Admirable Life of Sr Agnes* (2 vols, 1647) by a Benedictine of St Germain-des Prés who conducted the investigation at the request of M. Olier.

So 1665 saw the publication of that *Life* (Le Puy, 1 vol. in 4°, pp 666) by M. de Lantages, the erudition, historical probity and religious prudence of which were to attract enduring praise. These were three guiding qualities which governed the tripartite division of his work into (1) the testimonies and their criticism, (2) the biographical account, (3) the graces, visions and miracles of the heroine, for which he loosely follows the schema of the *Admirable Life* by the anonymous Benedictine. The Benedictine distinguished intellectual visions, real visions and representative visions, according to the current theory among contemporary specialists on mysticism. As for the title 'Venerable', which M. de Lantages introduced into his title, this did no more than consecrate existing practice, as the author explained in his long and interesting preface.

'For the rest, I have avoided calling her saint and blessed without qualification. And when, in referring to her, I use some terms which imply sanctity, this is merely to express that rare piety which made her venerable to all who knew her . . .'

'Some terms which imply sanctity'. Note the embarrassed language of M. de Lantages, who is evidently far from clear about the criteria and the 'model' to be followed to ensure the success of Agnes' cause. Often he combines visionary and miraculous phenomena throughout his account under the term 'extraordinary', which we find eight times in the preface alone.

In this form—apart from abridgments—the *Life of the Venerable . . .* according to M. de Lantages immediately enjoyed a popularity which is to be explained by its apologetic distribution by the three families concerned, the Dominicans, the Sulpicians and the Jesuits. M. de Lantages' biographer, M. Faillon, mentions several translations—into Latin in 1670, into German and Italian in 1672 and into Flemish in 1675, when the second French edition appeared. We may note that in 1675 the battles over Jansenism and quietism were at their height. The Dominicans and Jesuits of the Netherlands had no qualms about tossing Agnes' orthodoxy into the fray, guaranteed as it was by the Jesuit Papebroch and his team in Antwerp—the Bollandists—tireless in the collection of *Acta Sanctorum*. Agnes served the cause of the anti-Jansenists with the backing of Saint-Sulpice, this was to be the message naïvely expressed by Marie-Emma Lachaud, one of her nineteenth-century biographers: 'If our country ('Christian France') did not succumb totally to the Jansenist heresy, it is perhaps to her that we owe it.'[2] The edition of 1718 retouched certain of M. de Lantages' passages in order to be in total conformity with the bull *Unigenitus* of 1713.

But greater effort was going to be needed, and especially in the tribulations resulting from the different processes for Agnes' cause, of which we can do no more here than mention the stages.

2. VARIATIONS OF A HAGIOGRAPHIC FORTUNE (XVIIth-XXth CENTURIES)

(a) 1697-1749: *The consent of a people confronted by the new Roman Procedure*

It is difficult to determine at precisely what point the faculty of decreeing individual canonisations in their dioceses was withdrawn from bishops and reversed to the sovereign pontiff. Nevertheless the question seems to be settled with the decree of Urban VIII *Caelestis Hyerusalem cives,* of 5 July 1634,[3] in other words a few months before Agnes' death. This decree laid down, among other conditions, an interval of fifty years between the death and the preliminary examination of the cause.

In drawing up the diocesan cause in 1697 according to the rules of Urban VIII, surely Mgr d'Estaing de Saillans, bishop of Saint-Flour, was certain of winning the support of Rome? In 1700 the examination of the writings, the investigation of the reputation for sanctity and the absence of a public cult were verified, and on 16 June 1714 the cause was submitted by the Congregation of Rites to the pope, who approved it on 23 June.

Nothing was omitted to provide a dazzling demonstration of the consent of the French people to Agnes' beatification: petitions from the various religious orders, from several assemblies of the clergy, from Louis XIV himself (1702), from the Duchess of Burgundy (1703), from Cardinal de Noailles, later from Louis XV, who instructed his ambassador, Cardinal de Polignac, to hasten the conclusion of the cause in Rome. All the petitions exalt the same model: this Dominican Virgin 'has brought glory to the French Church . . . by bringing to the perfect life M. Olier, who laid the foundations of the seminary of Saint Sulpice . . . that purest of fountains from which several great bishops and an immense multitude of the lower clergy have successfully drawn a sincere piety, a sound doctrine, and a profound veneration and just obedience for the Apostolic See. . . .' The hints of ultramontane fidelity on the part of a nation suspected, in its clergy and its faithful, for its Gallicanism, are clear. In 'these sad times when faith has grown cold', political expediency reinforces the spiritual excellence of the cause: how could Rome be slow to understand the reasons for a popular devotion which can no longer be checked both in the diocese of Saint-Flour and in 'numerous other parts of the kingdom of France'?

The *promotor fidei,* Prospero Lambertini, seems to have proved particularly fastidious in this case. Did the future Benedict XIV, who was to give definitive form to the procedure for canonising saints, which to oppose his canonist's resistance to the pressure of a local church, in this case the church of France? Did not the man who was later sometimes called the 'pope of the Enlightenment' show a particular caution with regard to the 'extraordinary' phenomena which ran through Agnes' mystical life? Certain objections in the process would tend to confirm this hypothesis.

Whatever the reason, the process stopped in 1749, for want of money which neither Saint-Sulpice, which was to poor, nor the order of St Dominic, for reasons of jurisdiction over the convent at Langeac, would spend. The following stage was also to be marked by these twin perils, 'the excess of the supernatural' in Agnes' life and the money required to finance a new process.

(b) 1804-1808: *Mysticism on trial and the decree of 1808*

On the morrow of the French Revolution, which confirmed him in his role of director of conscience of the French clergy, M. Emery, superior general of Saint-Sulpice, wrote to M. Vernet, superior of the seminary of Viviers, whom he had sent as a delegate to Langeac: 'I have made up my mind to continue the process of Mother Agnes' beatification. The postulator of causes for the order of St Dominic said that £1,600 were necessary for the continuation. I have collected it, and the money has left for Rome. . . . I am placing the restoration of Saint-Sulpice under the protection of the Saint. . . .'[4]

The date is 1 September 1804 and, while M. Emery may think in his innocence that he has settled the question of finance, he knows that there must be a new life of his heroine in conformity with the century of the Enlightenment. The view is shared by Fr Joseph Faitot, ex-prior of the Dominicans of Saint Jacques in Paris, one of the leaders of the refractory Paris clergy alongside M. Emery. In two letters of 1805 he approves the recasting of Lantages' work, 'so far removed from what is required today that the three editions cause me more pain than pleasure.

'This vast mass of trivia presented as serious and cited as miracles, things which are really inexcusable presented as excesses of sanctity alongside others which indicate the hand of God and are really worthy of the respect which leads to wonder; a multitude of confidences which prove zeal and good faith without giving evidence of discernment. This is not what is required now, in a shrewd and perverse age. . . . (The task is no longer) to place Mother Agnes alongside St Teresa, but (to write) for truth and edification. . . . Who better than you, Monsieur. . . .'

In another letter Fr Faitot criticises the 1665 edition almost page by page and traces the new canvas:

'A particularly great virtue of this new work would be a fine exposition of the moral and mystical theology relating to the Christian virtues and the divine communications to the privileged soul. It would be impossible to criticise this little book for being nothing but a sermon or a theological treatise because this last part would in no way be forgotten. . . .'[5]

The lesson was perfectly understood by M. Emery, who lopped the 'excess of the supernatural' in order to 'return to history'. The result was the chapter he rewrote for the edition of 1808, which was still attributed to M. de Lantages, stressing the popular note. Agnes Galand is no longer the daughter of a 'master cutler', but of a simple 'cutler'. The model also becomes frankly apologetic, on the advice of the promotor of the cause, Fr Molineri, O.P., who explained to M. Emery in 1805 that it 'would be good to talk of the *benefit* which would result for the Catholic religion if France were given this new patron'.

But at the same time the postulator returned to more material considerations. He acknowledges receipt of the 293 Roman crowns: 'I hope this will be enough to hold the first Congregation on 3 October. If anything was lacking there, because of the increase in the price of chocolate as a result of the war, his eminence Cardinal Fesch has told me that he would supply it. . . .'

Napoleon's uncle, whom M. Emery had retaught to celebrate mass after the Revolution, was the most active agent in Rome, in his capacity as ambassador. In his Latin petition of 3 December 1805 he stresses to the consultors, not so much the fact that Mother Agnes 'brought M. Olier to the perfect life', as the eighteenth century had, but the reputation of the Society he had founded. Will Rome kindly honour Saint-Sulpice, a Society *'inviolata cathedrae Petri obedientia'*—translated: the only Congregation of priests free of any oath and a nursery of martyrs during the Revolution?

The political argument tells. M. Emery reduces the Dominican qualities of Mother Agnes and the 1808 edition makes her an openly Sulpician heroine, for 'the edification of the clergy'. Besides, as Fesch writes to him later, this edition is useless because the Italian edition of 1672 has been discovered in Rome 'and no one knew'! As a counterweight it will be necessary to supply the seventeen consultors with spices, sugar, chocolate and candles, of which the Continental blockade is depriving them. And the archives preserve a fresh note of expenditure, an additional £66 for a distribution of chocolate with which 'these Reverend Fathers are proving delighted'.[6]

So many pains were to be crowned by a half-success. On 19 March 1808 'His Holiness the Pope, according to the rites, announced the judgment. It is established that the Venerable Servant of God Agnes of Jesus so practised the virtues to a heroic degree that it is possible to proceed to the discussion of four miracles'. But, the decree adds, 'there are no eye-witnesses, only hearsay evidence, and therefore, according to the rules adopted by the Holy See, a greater number of miracles is required than in other causes before beatification can take place'.[7]

So much for the congratulations of the Boulogne priest-journalist, elevated to the See of Troyes the same year, who praised 'the editor for firmly forbidding us to mention more', for having, in the 1808 edition, 'for example suppressed the majority of the miracles reported (by M. de Lantages), not because there was doubt about their truth, but because it was thought better to limit ourselves to facts which instruct by edifying'![8]

(c) 1863-1963: *The revenge of the miraculous and ascetic and mystical theology*

Both out of the sensibility of an age which united romanticism and popular belief in miracles with a reinvigorated ultramontane loyalty and out of anxiety to bring to a successful conclusion a beatification short of miracles, the third generation of Agnes' hagiographers hastened to recover the 'excess of the supernatural' placed on the index by the wise and pious M. Emery.

Abbé Lucot gave a long explanation of the situation in the new (1863) edition of the *Life . . . by M. de Lantages* (Paris, 2 vols, 555 pp and 724 pp). Considerably revised and expanded by the addition of all the items from the various processes, this was to become the preferred edition, under the name Lantages-Lucot. Lucot apologised for the amputations in the 1808 edition: today 'many faithful souls, more and more disgusted by earthly life . . . love to multiply their connections with the Angels and the elect. . . . We are far from that time when criticism limited in a most parsimonious manner the gifts bestowed on the saints by infinite goodness' (p. XV).

Hence the important place given to visions, prophecies and to the role of angels in Agnes' life. As for her miracles, the Abbé Lucot on the one hand draws freely on the documents of the different processes for her beatification—and here he feels himself to be acting as a historian—and on the other emphasis is placed on the miracles which have a social value: the ending of the plague of 1630 in France, the end of a flood in the convent, the end of a great drought in Velay, Agnes' miraculous powers—very discreet in M. de Lantages' account: numerous cures, including some since 1856, according to the report of the Dominican General (vol. 2, Chaps XX and XXI). Moreover, Agnes' life 'was a continual miracle' (p. 448).

But the failure of 1808 has not been forgotten. While fully respecting the Dominican-Sulpician ambivalence of his heroine, Abbé Lucot clearly intends to confer on her that national dimension which she has so far lacked. Agnes is, and must be recognised as, a French saint. It is therefore necessary to make her 'popular'.

This was the purpose of *The Venerable Mother Agnes of Jesus* by Viscountess d'Ussel (Paris 1889). A noticeable feature is the unaccustomed sobriety of the title, which dispenses with the usual epithets, 'admirable' or 'marvellous' *Life*. The author, who donated the reliquary for the veneration of the nun at Langeac, proposes, by means of a purely historical account, to produce a portrait of a woman by a woman addressed . . . to all the women of France. There are, the author stresses for the first time (p. 324), two women in Agnes: '. . . alongside the ecstatic, the miracle-worker, have we sufficiently stressed the woman who talks, laughs, cries, acts like us, who lives our life . . .'.

Imitable because a woman like other women, Agnes still has to win her national renown by becoming 'popular', whence the *Popular Life of the Ven. Mother Agnes* (Le Puy 1894) by Abbé Césaire Sire. Breaking with its usual 'models', Teresa of Avila and Catherine of Siena, Agnes' life turns sharply towards Germaine Cousin, the sixteenth-century saint from Pébrac canonised in 1867. It is a striking metamorphosis at first sight, since St Germaine was a shepherd girl. . . . But the biographers like to recall that the daughter of the 'cutler' of Le Puy went to work at the bakery and was mocked, like St Germaine, for her 'bigotry' and her excessive generosity towards the poor. Marie-Emma Lachaud, in the same year, adds the popular miraculous element in her *Wonderful Life of the Venerable* . . . (Paris 1894). 'She was humble, simple, obedient . . . and, just as mountain remedies restore strength and health to bodies exhausted by excess, she was called God's humble flower', who barred the way to Jansenism yesterday and to freemasonry today: 'Agnes of Jesus is French and her sanctity has preserved the stamp of the generous and noble qualities which distinguish our country, but it has supernaturalised them.'

The fourth generation of Agnes' hagiographers reverses the perspective yet again. Reducing the 'Catholic and French' aspect of the nineteenth century, the twentieth century authors return to the speculative path on the basis of the Thomist data of ascetic and mystical theology. For the Sulpician R. Jeuné and for Fr Mortier,[9] Agnes must be understood as a contemplative and mystical religious in terms of St Teresa of Avila and St Catherine of Siena and in accordance with the Thomist doctrine as expounded principally in the works of Fr Garrigou-Lagrange. And in this way R. Jeuné justifies the 'extraordinary facts which have already found a place in this account. Others, even more surprising, will be reported later. Before continuing, the reader should call to mind the teachings of the faith: sanctifying grace is far superior to charisms'. But according to Fr Garrigou's *Christian Perfection and Contemplation,* if supernatural life remains, as it were, anaemic in the souls of 'ordinary' Christians, 'in the souls of saints, on the other hand, this supernatural life appears in all its energy, and it is this above all that we should consider in them, much more than the extraordinary, miraculous and inimitable gifts by which their sanctity is manifested to the outside world' (pp. 30-31).

It was left to the most recent biographer, Canon A. Müller, to sift this treatise on contemplation for which Agnes became the pretext. Using semantics and the works of Professor Lhermitte, the author presents clearly the problem of mysticism and of mystical language, of the danger of confusing hallucination, apparition and vision. He does not, however, like one branch of contemporary criticism, go so far as to raise the thorny problem of hysteria, though Lhermitte does deal with it. He concludes:

'Mother Agnes, for her part, never confused the privileges she enjoyed with sanctity; she always retained the sole preoccupation of seeking "the kingdom of God and its justice", fulfilling as exactly as possible the obligations of the religious life. That is the source of her influence' (p. 19).

And, perhaps, it is the beginning of another inquiry, the awareness saints have of themselves—and no longer the way in which they are perceived as such by the societies which harbour them.

A Saint for all ages

As we close (provisionally) the dossier of Mother Agnes, whose devotees still hope to bring the cause of her beatification to a successful end, three brief remarks seem appropriate.

The first is inspired by the plasticity of the 'model' through four centuries. These hagiographic variations can no doubt be explained by the personality of Agnes of Langeac, which is in the end fairly obscure and unobtrusive. It is thus easy to produce a composite portrait of her according to the needs of her cause and the tastes of a society, drawing inspiration from the great referencesstill invoked in the 'prayer author-ised by his lordship the bishop of Le Puy to ask for the beatification of Mother Agnes' (Langeac, 17 November 1907), notably Saints Agnes, Cecilia, Catherine of Siena and Rose of Lima.[10]

Nevertheless, and this is our second remark, the mutation of the model brings us up against one of the most formidable problems of Catholic sainthood, mysticism. In the approach to the phenomenon, the vagueness of the language, in the periodic embarrassment of hagiographers, it is clear that the problem of mysticism runs into the problem of historical criticism.

The compound of the natural and the supernatural leads us to think that a genuine shift was produced in the criteria of sanctity. The seven-teenth and twentieth centuries prefer an interior sanctity, one in which the 'supernatural' cannot create problems. The second half of the nineteenth century, on the other hand, showed us, through the miraculous a sanctity for external application. To become 'edifying' Agnes had to become 'miraculous', 'French' and 'popular', and here she is more Sulpician than Dominican. Miracles allow an apologetic for 'our age, dying of incredulity. It needs miracles to return to the God it has abandoned, who alone can heal it', wrote Maria Lachaud in her hagiography of 1894. That is almost word for word the definition of apologetics by miracle according to Cardinal Deschamps whose teaching triumphed at Vatican I. But then what is left of the real personality of Agnes?

Translated by Francis McDonagh

Notes

1. The printed and the manuscript sources dealing with the life of Agnes of Jesus are listed in A. Müller *Une mystique dominicaine du XVIIe siècle: la Vénérable Mère Agnes de Langeac* (Monastère Sainte-Catherine de Langeac, Haute-Loire 1963) pp. 27-29.

2. Marie-Emma Lachaud, *Vie merveilleuse de la Vénérable Mère Agnes de Jésus* (Paris 1894) preface.

3. On this long controversy, see 'Canonisation dans l'Eglise Romaine' *Dict. Théol. Cath.* cols 1633-36.

4. 'Archives of Saint-Sulpice' *Documents Emery* VIII, 8674.

5. *Ibid.*, XI, 212-13; 239-40.

6. *Ibid.*, 'Letters from Fesch to Emery' XI, 163; 217; 223; 431.

7. 'Decree of the prefect of the Congregation of Rites, Della Somaglia' *Journal des Curés* 72 (20 May 1908).

8. *Mélanges de Philosophie* vol. 6 (1809) pp. 357-63.

9. M. R. Jeuné *Une mystique dominicaine, la Vénérable Agnès de Langeac* (Paris 1924); R. P. D. A. Mortier *La Vénérable Mère Agnes de Langeac* (Paris 1925).

10. Quoted by Jeuné, *op. cit.* pp. 240-41.

Eduardo Hoornaert

Models of Holiness Among the People

THE VATICAN authorities have for many centuries—and especially since the Council of Trent—used a model of holiness on which they have based their criteria for canonisation. The very term 'canonisation' points to the existence of objective norms, rules or 'canons' used in such cases by the curia. On the other hand, however, it is well known that certain people have always been venerated by the people as a whole and such 'canonisations by the people' are as old as the Church itself. These popular saints are sometimes local and transitory in character, but some of them are much more lasting and universal. Two clear examples of such popular figures are John XXIII, who was regarded by certain sectors of the Catholic people as a saint, and Pope John Paul I, who acquired a reputation for sanctity during his short period of office.

The question that arises in this context is this: Is this merely an impression, a popular feeling or an expression of popular religiosity, or is there something of structural importance underlying it? Is it simply a smile, a gesture or way of behaving which causes the people to react in this way or does this type of canonisation by the people point to a definite model? Can we, in other words, discover a criterion or a structure in it? This is an important question, because, in the last resort, it amounts to a value-judgement on the part of the people of God that is always in danger of being given a negative evaluation by those who are responsible for the organisation of the Christian religion. Yet surely the people of God are themselves the guarantors of all plans for the future and it is they who evolve the Church's strategy and provide the driving force for the history of Christianity. I should like to consider this question in the light of the history of the Church in Brazil. I shall begin by looking at three popular 'saints' who have not been canonised by the Church and then go on to consider, on the basis of these three men, the whole theme of the model of holiness among the people.

1. THREE POPULAR SAINTS IN THE HISTORY OF THE CHURCH IN BRAZIL

São Sepé is a little town in the state of Rio Grande do Sul in the south of Brazil. It is on the river of the same name and near the much bigger town of Santa Maria. The name São Sepé was given by the people to the place where the Indian missionary Christian, José Tiaraju, was murdered in 1756 by the united Spanish and Portuguese demarcation forces on the bank of the river that had been named by him.[1] (These troops had the task of driving the Indian Christians from the east bank of the Paraguay river in accordance with the treaty of Madrid of 1750.) The people at once 'canonised' José Tiaraju and this canonisation has continued for more than two hundred years, although it has remained fairly local.[2]

The life of Cícero Romão Batista, the holy priest of Juazeiro in the southern part of the eastern state of Brazil, Ceará, must be situated within a completely different context. Padre Cícero came in 1872 to the very poor village of Jauzeiro in the parish of Crato as a newly ordained priest. He stayed there for sixty-two years until his death in 1934. The chapel there was dedicated to Our Lady of the Seven Sorrows, but the young assistant priest had a remarkable devotion to Our Lady of the Rosary, who was the patron saint of slaves in Brazil. Padre Cícero prayed every day with his slaves before the statue of Our Lady of the Rosary, using the prayer of the rosary. His fame spread very quickly among the people working on the great cattle breeding farms in the Ceará and in north-east Brazil in general. Pilgrims came from all parts to Juazeiro,[3] which separated in 1911 from the mother town of Crato and quickly developed into one of the biggest towns in the interior of Brazil. The 'pilgrims of Padre Cícero' still regard Juazeiro as a holy city.[4]

The third popular saint whom I would like to mention in this article is the Italian Capuchin Frei Damião de Bozzano, who has been travelling in the interior of north-east Brazil and is still active in popular missions. He is practically the only remaining popular missionary who is continuing the Capuchin tradition initiated in the beginning of the eighteenth century. Most missionaries who are Europeans or who have been trained in accordance with European models have a very secularising attitude towards the Brazilian people and have tended in the long run to lose touch with them. Frei Damião, on the other hand, was welcomed by the people and regarded as a saint by them, almost from the beginning of his ministry. The sermons that he has gone on repeating have been translated from the Italian and consist of dogmatic or moral statements drawn from the type of Catholic theology that was taught at the Gregorian University in the late 1920s. He is criticised by the more progressive Catholics working in Brazil, who accuse him of being manipulated by right-wing politicians. What cannot, however, be disputed is that his presence in any town that he visits for a few days transforms the place into a centre of encounter, friendship and happiness.[5]

2. POPULAR HOLINESS, COLONIAL SLAVERY AND FANATICISM

Two factors that are common to all three cases of popular holiness discussed above strike us at once. In the first place, the popular saint would seem to appear in Brazil in a special relationship with slavery and, in the second place, he would also seem to arouse fanaticism among the people.

The Brazilian popular saint is primarily different from his fellow-men in that he in one way or another rejects colonial slavery. 'Colonial slavery'[6] in this context should not be confused with ordinary slavery, which is above all a juridical concept denoting a typical form of private ownership, in which the slave is not accepted in the legal sense as a personality by the community and therefore belongs completely to his master. Juridical slavery of this kind has not existed in Latin America since 1888. Slavery, however, still exists in a deeper economic sense and has been given the name of 'colonial slavery'.

It is an indisputable fact that, since the sixteenth century, Europeans and other peoples have managed to carry out their plans in Latin America only by imposing compulsory labour on the original so-called 'Indian' population and on labour forces imported from Africa. The stimulus for this compulsory labour sometimes came from outside, for example, from torture, imprisonment or legal slavery, but it was and is also caused by economic conditions such as very low rewards for work done. Most people who have studied the question agree that certain forms of colonial slavery have continued to exist in Latin America.

I do not intend to discuss this question in detail here, but would like to point to the fact that the popular saints to whom I referred above have all, in one way or another, taken up a distinctive position with regard to colonial slavery. São Sepé fought to the death to set his people free from slavery. Padre Cícero tried to evolve an alternative, non-colonial form of agriculture[7] and Frei Damião differs from most other priests in his attitude of extreme patience towards the descendants of slavery and those who have inherited the tradition of colonial slavery. We shall be considering this question later in this article.

We have already mentioned the fanaticism aroused among the Brazilian people by these popular saints. The term occurs again and again in any description of their lives and activities. The veneration of São Sepé is generally regarded as legendary and tendentious in Church circles, since it is for the most part the missionaries who were murdered by the 'Indians', not those murdered by the Europeans, and certainly not the Indian Christians murdered by Europeans, who are venerated as martyrs. The veneration of Padre Cícero is even nowadays usually dismissed by the clergy as an expression of the people's backwardness, ignorance or fanaticism. Most parish priests working in the interior either manipulate or reject the missionary tours of Frei Damião and very few believe that his missions have any value as such.

If the term 'fanaticism', as used in this context, is examined more closely, it becomes clear that it is not the people who call themselves fanatical—others describe them as such. The term is therefore related in a special sense to the social situation of the Brazilian people in society. It is possible that speaking about fanaticism defines and situates not the object about which one is speaking, but the subject who is speaking. In using the term 'fanaticism', in other words, an attempt is made to reduce the phenomenon of the people and indeed the whole of popular religiosity to the level of emotion and this attempt is made from the vantage point of those sectors of society which are dominant. Speaking about fanaticism is, in other words, an attempt to reduce the reality, which includes a refusal to consider certain factors and to allow the others—in this case, the Brazilian people—to express themselves. If these others, the fanatics who follow Frei Damião, were allowed to speak, what would they say? And what would Frei Damião himself have to say about it?

3. THE MODEL OF HOLINESS OF THE BRAZILIAN PEOPLE

It is only as an alternative, that is, either as a threat or as a sign of hope, that the European or the North American presence in Latin America from the sixteenth century until the present can be seen by the Brazilian people. Insofar as they have identified themselves with colonialism, the Europeans and North Americans have constituted a threat to the subjected sectors of the population of Brazil. This threat has been so great that the history of the original Brazilian Indian population has been a history of extermination. The country has been set free from the Indians and made open to the Europeans and North Americans, so that these could exploit it by perpetuating colonial slavery. At the same time, the Catholic religion has also been a very effective threat to the native Indians and the slaves imported from Africa.[8]

Not all the Europeans and North Americans, however, who have come to Brazil have identified themselves with colonialism. Those who went as missionaries among the people certainly did not. Such men as Feliciano Mendes and Lourenço de Nossa Senhora in Minas Gerais sold their slaves and their property or land, that had been bestowed on them by the state, and became hermits, living among the people.[9] The Breton Capuchin Martin of Nantes and the well-known Jesuit, Antonio Vieira, in Maranhao, defended the freedom of the Indians in opposition to the European owners of landed property and slave-traders.[10] In refusing to identify themselves in this way with the colonial pattern of behaviour, these men made it possible for the holiness of the Brazilian people to be realized. In other words, holiness can only be really understood in relation to a concrete historical sacrilege.

The great sacrilege that has been committed from the sixteenth century onwards by Europeans and North Americans is the establishment of slavery, both in its legal and in its colonial form, in the world. The people of Brazil, sanctified by the Holy Spirit, have been deeply desecrated by this act of sacrilege. Colonial slavery has become the lord of the people of Brazil, the country and its history. This country and its history have to some degree been restored to their primitive holiness by the popular saints of Brazil. Juazeiro has been transformed, for example, from a village of slaves into a 'holy city' by the presence of Padre Cícero and the mother town of Crato, which is powerfully orientated towards slavery of the colonial kind, is dialectically opposed to it. This new dialectical relationship between Juazeiro and Crato has, in a sense, placed Brazil in a new way at the disposal of the people. It is no longer a country in which people are related solely as masters and slaves—it is also a place where people meet each other as pilgrims. The world is not simply a closed space—it is open to an alternative use.

São Sepé has done something similar in Rio Grande do Sul. The colonial powers of Spain and Portugal regarded the Rio Grande exclusively as a place of colonial trade. It was important for Spain that the Rio de la Plata should be made free for colonial shipping routes and for Portugal that the Rio Grande should be open to the slave trade of São Paulo. The treaty of Madrid of 1750 made it possible for seven flourishing Indian missionary stations to be exchanged for Colonia do Sacramento, a centre of smuggling.[11] This transaction, exchanging one place for others, was a basic misunderstanding of the country of Brazil which was given 'by God and Saint Michael'[12] to the missionary Christians.[13] It was in this alternative use of the country that the great historical vocation of Rio Grande do Sul was to be found. It was to be a holy country, given to people for them to live there in freedom, peace and love. It was also São Sepé who revealed this to Brazil, when he defined Brazil as a holy place.

History has also been revealed in Brazil by the popular saints. Frei

Damião's visits to various places and villages in north-east Brazil have led to a new use of time everywhere in the country, a use that is in striking contrast to the older, everyday use of it. It has achieved in a special way what is also achieved by religious feasts. There is, in other words, an alternation between 'holy' and 'sacrilegious' times. During the latter, the bodies of the poor people are fully exploited by the rich. Frei Damião's visits restore their bodies and souls by restoring time. This simple fact of giving time to meet God and one's fellow-men is the great and positive achievement of the popular missions.

It is not possible to discuss here the important question as to how efficient these attempts to restore time and place are. All that we can do is to point out that, however limited they may be, these attempts are made and that they form part of a conscious or unconscious popular strategy with far-reaching consequences. In this context, the popular saint is above all someone who reveals the holiness of God's Spirit as active among the people. He is involved in a popular strategy of resistance, restoration, reorganisation and identification. The people need such saints if they are to rediscover themselves and transcend the effects of sacrilege. Colonial slavery results in the destruction of communities and the production of atomised individuals. The popular saint, working slowly and patiently, restores the unity and community of the people on the basis of traditional and religious elements. His action, however, is temporary and relative. He is not a hero who is able to go beyond and above the achievements of the people and the point of balance is not to be found in his individual virtues, but in the fact that he opts for people. He is, in a word, the temporary and relative expression of the people of God sanctifying themselves. This is evident from the relationship established by the people of north-east Brazil between Padre Cícero and Frei Damião. When Padre Cícero died in 1934 and Frei Damião began to travel round the country from 1931 onwards, the latter was almost at once regarded as continuing in the tradition of Padre Cícero. This transference is not really from one individual to another, but rather a transference of task. Frei Damião is clearly not free from serious limitations and his message is manipulated by politicians. This points to the temporary nature of his historical significance. We may therefore conclude that the popular saint is in no sense a hero or an exceptional figure who stands head and shoulders above the people. He is, on the contrary, the one who, as it were, carries in himself the vocation of the people.

A further conclusion is that a definite model of holiness can only be placed over and against a definite example of sacrilege which violates the people of God. The popular saint reveals the holiness of the people who are inspired by the Spirit of God.

4. CAN THIS MODEL OF HOLINESS ONLY BE APPLIED TO LATIN AMERICA?

The reader may perhaps have a rather exotic impression of the three Brazilian saints whose activities have been briefly described above. It cannot be denied that such travelling missionaries as Frei Damião are seldom encountered nowadays in Europe or North America, with the result that the suspicion inevitably arises that these popular saints are a typically Latin American phenomenon and will, in view of the rapid progress of mankind, soon disappear from the scene. It is, of course, true that the symbolic expressions of popular Latin American religiosity give a traditionally medieval impression, but it is at the same time important to make a distinction between the symbolic aspect—the processions, pilgrimages, novenas and feasts—and the reality signified by these symbols. And the reality or realities to which the symbols point are neither exotic nor antiquated.

Since the sixteenth century, the world has effectively become one. This movement began with its centre in Spain and Portugal, from which an Atlantic empire was established. It later extended to the Netherlands, France, England and finally to North America, each of which occupied the central position in turn. Throughout various periods of economic and political change, Catholicism—and particularly Iberian Catholicism—continued to be the great formative power influencing the development of colonialism in Latin America. Colonial slavery, which forms the basis on which popular holiness has to be interpreted, is therefore to be regarded not as a typically Latin American phenomenon, but rather as a universally Catholic phenomenon. The model of holiness that is found among the Latin American people is in the first place a protest against Europe, the motherland of Catholicism, the type of Catholicism that was transplanted into Latin American soil.

What has to be done quite urgently is to investigate this accusation against European Catholicism and to examine the relationship between Catholicism and colonialism. We have to consider very carefully the statement that Catholicism in the poor parts of the world has often been and still is a sacrilegious religion, promoting the slave-trade in Africa[14] and colonial slavery in Latin America[15] and still supporting colonialism even today. Africa and Latin America reveal Europe to itself. It is difficult for Europeans to recognise the seamy side of history without the help of this revelation and this seamy side shows us the inevitable results of gain and capitalism, the slave-trade and slave-labour and a continuing form of colonial slavery.

In the second place, the Latin American model of holiness may well be less exotic than it seems to be at first sight. This exoticism is within our own experience, not entirely outside it. Popular religiosity exists everywhere. Sometimes it is difficult to recognise, but it is a fact that Catholicism is a complex dialectical reality. We must consider this question in the next section.

5. POPULAR HOLINESS AND POPULAR RELIGION

Throughout the whole history of the Church, relationships have never been entirely harmonious and there has always been a 'social' question within the Church. As an expression of this, a group of those responsible for the organisation of life in the Church succeeded in making use of the word and everything that it signified in terms of power and in forming a central culture on the basis of it. In this way, they came to constitute one pole of Catholicism. The other pole has always been popular Catholicism. Those who form the first pole have always tended to regard this other pole as popular religiosity, characterised as ignorance, passivity or, in the case of the phenomenon of the popular saint, fanaticism.

The people, however, have always had their own means of communicating their religiosity in non-verbal and corporeal expressions. The members of the central, clerical hierarchy of the Church have conducted a continuous action of repression, at the same time accompanied by an attempt to manipulate and reorganise the atomised elements of popular Catholicism and thus bring them within the hierarchical system. It is therefore impossible to find popular Catholicism in a pure form. It has always to be situated within a wider arena, although there is a risk that it will, in this case, be misunderstood. In other words, there is an interiorisation of official or clerical Catholicism that within popular Catholicism, with the result that the latter appears, at least superficially, as an ambiguous phenomenon. The elements of popular Catholicism can only be correctly understood in relation to the opposite pole in the Church, the hierarchy. Seen from this pole, popular religiosity seems to be deprived of all inner structure and completely dependent on the authoritative aspects of the Church.

There is a relationship between the two aspects, but there is not always a dependence. The relationship is a dialectical one and it is part of the popular strategy to keep it at a vague and consciously ambiguous level. There is also, however, an unconscious ambiguity, because many people have lost their popular feeling and have completely absorbed the hierarchical model. The popular model of holiness, which is, of course, in many respects quite different from the canonical model, is a clear indication of the fact that the popular religion is not an amorphous 'religiosity', but a structured reality. Its structures originate mainly from a communal experience of the same history and it is therefore very difficult to understand the popular saint without an experience of the history of the people. The 'miracle' of liberation from slavery is not a miracle for someone who has never experienced slavery. Not only slavery, but also other historical sacrileges give rise to popular saints and popular fanaticism. Every historical situation is characterised by a tension between holiness and sacrilege and the popular saint is the expression of that tension. He is not of marginal, but of central importance in the Church, because he places his finger on the sore spot—that the Church has to be converted to itself and that the hierarchy has to be converted to the people of God. The popular saint is an appeal to conversion from the constantly recurring danger of pharisaism of official religion.

These considerations should not lead us to make an idol of popular religion, since this would be as dangerous as an uncritical acceptance of clericalism in the Church. Many members of the clergy take the side of the people here and thus favour polarisation in the Church into two distinct groups. On the other hand, many members of the people favour the clerical structure of the Church and allow themselves to be used in polarisation in the opposite direction. It is therefore necessary to distinguish between the spirits here and this is in practice not easy.

Let me give a concrete example of this. It is part of the strategy of the central culture to present a saint as a hero who stands head and shoulders above ordinary human beings. In this way, his image is particularised and he thus ceases to be an expression of the people of God. Such a model of holiness, as a product of the central culture of the Church, is to a great extent interiorised by the people and is a typical example of a recuperation of the popular culture by the central culture of the Church. The politicians of Juazeiro were the first to have a great statue of Padre Cícero erected, not to provide a visible representation of popular holiness for the people, but rather in order to islolate Padre Cícero by placing him literally head and shoulders above the people and making a distinction in this way between the town of Juazeiro and the saint. Every representation of a saint is subject to such forms of manipulation and recuperation. There is no pure model of holiness outside the arena of concrete human society. No human authority can therefore absolve us from our need to think critically, above all with regard to models of holiness.

Translated by David Smith

Notes

1. Aurélio Porto *História das Missões Orientais do Uruguay* I and II (Porto Alegre 1954) *passim.* See also Eliezer Pacheco *O Povo Condenado* (Rio de Janeiro 1977), who provides a good bibliography.

2. *Sepé* is a Guarani word meaning 'leader of his people' or 'counsellor of his people'.

3. The word used in this context is not 'pilgrims', but the Portuguese *romeiros* or 'Rome travellers'.

4. Ralph della Cava *Miracle at Joaseiro* (New York 1970) has provided quite a good introduction to the whole problem surrounding Padre Cícero, together with a full bibliography. Anyone wishing to go more deeply into the question, however, should consult such Brazilian authors as Amália Xavier de Oliveira. H. Groenen's doctoral thesis *Schisma zwischen Kirche und Volk* (Nijmegen 1978) gives a good, recent account.

5. Abdalaziz de Moura *Frei Damião e os impasses da religião popular* (Petrópolis 1977).

6. Jacob Gorender *O escravismo colonial* (São Paulo 1978). The concept 'colonial slavery' has been analysed in detail in contemporary Brazilian studies.

7. Sylvio Rabello *Os artesãos do Padre Cícero* (Recife 1967).

8. Eduardo Hoornaert *Formação do catolicismo brasileiro* (Petrópolis 1978²), especially the first chapter.

9. *História da Igreja no Brasil, Primeira época* (Petrópolis 1977) pp. 104-109.

10. *Ibid.* pp. 115-118.

11. Eliezer Pacheco *op. cit.*

12. These words were spoken by São Sepé in an address to the demarcation troops.

13. In Latin American mission literature, a distinction is made between *missioneiro* (missionary Christian) and *missionário* (missionary).

14. J. Heyke 'Er zijn daar veel slaven en olifanten' *Tijdschrift voor Theologie* 2 (1978) 158-178.

15. For the relationship between slave-labour and baptism, see *História da Igreja no Brasil, Primeira época* (Petrópolis 1977) pp. 302-307.

Claudio Leonardi

From 'Monastic' Holiness
to 'Political' Holiness

FOR MANY centuries the model of holiness was the monk. From the fourth to the twentieth century Christians thought of the perfect imitation of Christ as the monastic life, but now this image is worn out.

We can account for its beginning and its ending by an historical understanding of the phenomenon of holiness. Holiness is the process of union with Christ through the Spirit. It is a process and fulfilment, meaning a transformation of the person which takes place in history.

There can be no material awareness of the process of deification because the body is united with the divine but also different from it in time, it is already divine but not yet. The process by which man becomes God is not theologically knowable because we do not 'know' the two polarities of this process: history and the Spirit. But at least we can know the history of the language used to express this process of deification. Not by material awareness but symbolic.

We speak of models of holiness but the term must be used with caution, because the only model of holiness is Christ (and the Virgin Mary) and all others are not models but secondary models, and because we cannot make an abstract schema of perfection which we can know and describe in advance: holiness does not mean possessing God but being possessed by him. It is the Spirit who leads to the Father in Christ and the Spirit blows where he will.

So rather than speaking of models we should speak of the language of deification. When this is experienced it appears in history and finds expression: the divinity revealed is knowable and so is the oneness with God experienced. We can say that the time of the Church, between the first and the second coming of Christ is the time during which the awareness of becoming God is revealed in more developed language: the concept is refined and the experience of God is deepened.

We can speak of the history of holiness as the history of the Christian language of holiness. For this the writings of the saints, their actions and life stories, the figures they represent and the art they inspire are central to the making of this history.

Before there was monastic language there was the language of the martyrs. This was the first language of Christian perfection.

The letter of Diognetes describes the condition of Christians before the fourth century.[1] What struck the pagans was the Christians' detachment from the world and their lack of fear of death (1, 1). This was possible because the Word of truth infused into them had become their life (12, 7). This life was different from natural life and had its own laws (5, 10), which made Christians live as strangers upon earth (5, 5). But the Christians were no different from other people in any external way, they did not live in different cities, they did not speak a different language, wear different clothes or follow a special human teaching (5, 1-2).

This life finds its place in history when it is proved by martyrdom: the Christian shows that he is different from others when he confronts the power of the state, which represents public history. Perfection is seen as the conquest of death. The Christian is the one who suffers pain and death but discovers in death the fulness of life.

Felicity is in prison. She is in labour and suffers great pain. The guard says: If you are suffering so much now, what will you feel like when you face the wild beasts. Felicity answers: Now it is I who suffer but then another will suffer in me for me, because I will suffer for him.[2] This is the language of martyrs: the substitution of one person for another, the transformation of the human person into a person both human and divine, Christ, takes place at the moment of sacrifice. The martyr gives up his life and receives in exchange the divine life, the Trinity appears in him.[3] Divine power is infused into the martyr, which is manifested as victory over death, the passing from human pain to divine joy.

The language of this ontological transformation is still quite crude, because deification is seen as materialising in the body. The language of martyrs corresponds to baptismal language and only expresses the beginning of Christian life: baptism does not yet express the problem of a life to be lived in the world but not of the world.

It is this problem that the monastic model tries to solve and which is the basis of its new language: how to conquer not death, but the world; how to build within nature and history the human-divine, how baptism can continue throughout life. The monk is the perfect follower of Christ because he conquers the world by dying to the world.

The monastic model is a continuation of the martyr model because it sees ontological transformation in the passover from cross to resurrection. Since it raises and tries to deal with the difficult problem of the possibility of the human-divine in history, monastic language is superior to the language of martyrs.[4]

Christian monasticism became an historical event in the fourth century with the coming of the age of Constantine. With Constantine and Theodosius the ancient world became Christian, not because of a general conversion but by a change of cult. This caused a serious crisis in the Church. Perfection was not a goal that could be set for a people who had simply changed cult and not their lives. Political power always governs human life and now it was assuming Christian symbols. For Eusebius of Caesarea, the historical presence of Christ, his authority (*exousia*) was entrusted to the emperor. This was the beginning of Christendom, the period during which the civil structures were constituted in reference to Christian values, and power was ideologically justified in Christ.

In this situation martyrdom became impossible and the hagiographic model sought new forms. Monasticism had the merit of creating the historical possibility of perfection during the period of Christendom; it demonstrated that a life which was different from natural historical life, a life which was both historical and divine was perfectly possible. Monasticism developed a language expressing a higher view of Christ than the language of martyrs. It saw death to the world as the material abandonment of history, but also taught that refusing pagan worship was not enough to make divine charity appear in history. What is required is a more intense and long-term witness, a new morality: new relationships with God, neighbours and self.

This monastic achievement took place by abandoning history to the Christian State. Thus monasticism gave up the idea of perfection for the ordinary faithful: perfection was for the few, a closed shop, which set up a division in the body of the Church between perfect and imperfect, designated by physical separation.

The figure of the monk, with its merits and limitations is the only image of holiness expressing the deification of man in the age of Constantine. So of course it dominated the history of perfection up till now, when Christendom is coming to an end.

The story of Constantinian Christendom took place chiefly in the Eastern churches where imperial power remained supreme. Here the monastic language of deification was faithfully preserved and the exclusion of the perfect from history was also rigorously maintained. Hence in the East, the Plotinian and gnostic tendencies found it easier to emerge and they were very influential upon the rise and continuance of monasticism: flight from the world to rise towards the One, the world seen as imperfect. Origen's view of man was the monastic one: the body is a diminishment of the soul. Irenaus' view that the body is capable of deification remained in the background.[5]

Athanasius and Jerome in their biographies of Anthony, Hilarion and Paul set limits on the gnostic element in Coptic and Syrian monasticism. But this limitation was more clearly defined in the transfer to the West of the monastic ideal effected by Cassian at the beginning of the fifth century: he diluted Origenism by an injection of Pelagianism. Thus with Cassian the superiority of the cenobite to the hermit was established. The monk lived by a common rule and his duty was ascesis: contemplation was a pure gift but it required an effort at ascesis. Ascesis was the school for perfection: anyone who was not a monk was like a pagan. In order to justify this drastic choice, Cassian was obliged to accept the myth of the apostolic origin of monasticism.[6]

This potentially heretical ideological justification did not prevent Eastern and Western monasticism from expressing a fully orthodox hagiographic model displaying a highly developed experience of God, as shown by Simeon the New Theologian and William of St Thierry. The saint was the person who renounced the world for God and to show the world that it was possible to live for a reality that is greater than the world. The fulness of union with God through the Holy Spirit was found in these two men.

Soon the monastic model was forced to adapt its static position towards history. In the West the Roman Empire fell to the Germans: in the face of this apocalypse Christians were obliged to rethink their attitude to the world. They could ot simply avoid the world, they had to cope with it and try to convert it; they became involved in history.

Already Ambrose had stood out against the Emperor Theodosius. In Africa Augustine was present when Vandals destroyed his church but ordered his faithful to stay put. Thus from the fifth and sixth centuries on the Western monastic ideal was broadened. The saint was still someone who renounced the world (a monk) but the monk's duty was not only cenobitic ascesis but also the conversion of the people. Salvian of Marseilles proclaimed prophetically that Constantinian Christianity was not Christian and he himself, like Augustine, was a model of perfection as a bishop living a monastic life, an apostle who preached and built up part of Christ's body, the Church in history. Shortly afterwards Hilary of Arles declared that the perfect monk mystically received the fulness of priesthood, his life was wholly apostolic before the office of bishop was legally conferred upon him.

Thus the monastic model came back into contact with history; a monk had a mission as well as a cenobitic vocation. The Western Church was not just a Church of monks but also of the people. The model of Africa and Arles was taken up by Rome: Gregory the Great expressed in his life and work the hagiographic model of a monk who remained a monk even when he was involved in history. History became what the monk had a duty to convert. The saint was the person who brought God to history and proclaimed the Church as God's historical home. For Gregory the bishop was the heir of the Old Testament prophets.[7]

During the Middle Ages in the West, history was no longer only the space occupied by the Christian State: in the West the Constantinian formula could not stand, in spite of the latter day effort of Charlemagne. As perfection was expressed in the saint who existed in history, its language was both mystical and prophetic, prophecy which measured history against meta-history. Columba and Boniface were the prophet-evangelists of the German world, Bede set Anglo-Saxon history within the biblical vision.[8]

The medieval West was not a Constantinian age but rather a Gelasian age. Christendom changed: the historical power of Christ was not linked with the power of the emperor or king, but was manifest through the power of the Church, the pope and bishops or laity.[9] The first obvious appearance of this Christly authority was not in Merovingian hagiography but in the Carolingian episcopate which stood out against the power of king and emperor.[10]

In the history of Christian language Gregory VII represents the moment in which eschatological power was opposed to sacral power. Gregory held that the historical opposition between the two powers was essential for the making of an image of perfection not confined to flight from the world, but which also suffered defeat through its inability to control history by ecclesiastical power. Thus he invoked Christ's eschatological kingship over and above the power of the pope.

After a thousand years of Christian experience the eleventh century brought a change: the opposition between the two powers consolidated Gelasian Christianity but it was also a struggle which weakened both powers and led to their downfall.

Christendom, that is the justification of civil and ecclesiastical power by the authority of Christ, remained the condition to which perfection was subject. The only possible model of perfection remained the monk, who was separated from nature and the world by physical barriers. But, with the turn of the millennium Christians became increasingly aware that the high Middle Ages' attempt to construct history in terms of meta-history had not fully succeeded.

Between the eleventh and sixteenth centuries this awareness grew: the desire for perfection could no longer be seen as taking over the world. The heritage of St Augustine was confronted with the fact that Christianity was a failed revolution. The distance between (Constantinian or Gelasian) Christendom and faith was only too plain. Bernard of Clairvaux made a strenuous effort to restore the figure of the missionary monk, but without success. In order to survive, the monastic ideal had to be expanded again. The monk should not flee the world or take over the world by converting it: he must love the world.

Francis of Assisi exemplified this new model. He abandoned the idea of Christian conquest, and refused to use anything but the word and the cross. In him monasticism rediscovered the total renunciation of the world. But this time there were no gnostic elements. Francis was not only wholly apostolic and missionary, he loved nature and history as well as people. This new approach was possible because Francis had understood the meaning of eschatological fulfilment: he saw the final goal of nature and history.[11] Thus the monastic model derived from Augustine was completed: abandoning the world also meant loving the world. But the completion of the monastic model was the beginning of its end.

Monasticism survived because Francis succeeded in giving the friars minor a rule which distinguished them within the society of the Church. Monasticism also survived Christendom because Francis loved nature and history but did not try to cope with the problem of history. He affirmed the primacy of the Spirit and the cross (the stigmata), the primacy of the person and the innocent victim, but he did not see that this primacy involved an historical confrontation.

Francis was a powerful Christ-like figure. He summed up one monastic tradition and opened up another. His influence remained till modern times. The great Carmelite mystics were in his footsteps, they developed the awareness of the divine in the human person and direct guidance by God. In Thérèsa of Lisieux, the culmination of the Carmelite tradition, Francis' renunciation of the world became absolute. Thérèsa not only renounced political action but also the Word as a means of relating to the world; in her, perfection was not revealed in any historical action. But this was not simply a renunciation of the world. Her awareness of being consumed by love for God through the Spirit included the longing for the world to share in this love. Rather than renunciation, this longing was the saint's way of relating to history.[12]

This was the final stage of the Franciscan tradition and the end of a whole history of the hagiographic figure. There was no possible higher expression of the love of God than self-annihilation like the Word. In Thérèsa deification meant complete crucifixion. The stigmata on Francis' body were felt by Thérèsa in her soul, as was shown by her experience of atheism. But when union with Christ becomes so total at the psychological level, external signs of separation from the world become superfluous. With Thérèsa of Lisieux, the monastic model comes full circle.

This marks the end of a whole period in the history of the Church. The figure of the monk as necessary for Christian perfection arose in the presence of a secular power which claimed, in the pagan tradition, to be the apex of history, and which accepted the principles of the faith as norms for its political institutions. The figure of perfection could not coincide with this; hence the monastic separation. But this state of affairs no longer operates. The great empires which now rule the world do not claim the justification of Christian principles. Christendom is over and we are now living in a post-Christian era.[13]

Now the figure of the martyr appears to have common characteristics with that of the monk. The martyr is separated from the world by death, the monk is separated from nature. The idea of (Constantinian or Gelasian) Christendom is inadequate to explain the development of hagiographic language, if it is not set in the wider context of the concept of ecclesial *kairos* (time). Martyr and monk are the type of holiness during the time of the Church marked by confrontation with the Gentiles.

Since the time of the apostles up till today, the Church has had to face paganism. The Jewish people who were waiting for the Messiah did not preach to the Gentiles. Thus according to Paul, the Church began the time of the Gentiles and their incorporation in Christ. This time does not cover the whole history of the Church because, when it is over, the time for the conversion of Israel begins.

The Church's confrontation with the Gentiles revolves round the Gentiles' supreme value, nature. Thus renunciation of life (by the martyr) or history (by the monk) represents a single ideal of holiness during the time of the Gentiles. Confrontation with the Gentiles means coming to terms with a history in which nature is accepted as a firm and certain datum. Only the power of the Holy Spirit can liberate from nature. This makes it understandable that Origen was valued higher than Irenaus, and the Constantinian or Gelasian doctrine higher than Augustine. Spiritualism and temporalism are two sides of the same coin.

Awareness given by the Holy Spirit of our own humanity as human and divine, of our own freedom of choice which does not need sacral mediations of power; awareness of the spiritual community as a historical guide are the results of a long period during which the Gentile tradition played its part as a necessary adversary. Because the Church has continually affirmed that divine-human perfection is possible through the primacy of the person, the primacy of the Spirit, the idea of the person as an absolute value was an achievement of medieval and modern times.

At the spiritual level this means the primacy of the mystic, at the historical level the awareness of history as antagonistic to the person, the impossibility of accepting nature as a certain datum, of being part of this immutable nature and subject to any power whatever, however justified. Thus our own time, the end of the second millennium, has come to the end of the confrontation between the Church and the Gentiles.[14]

A period has come to an end, the monastic model is no longer viable, the relationship with history can no longer be stated in terms of Christendom. We can no longer accept nature as a value, it can no longer satisfy us as persons in any way; no power, culture or natural authority can bring fulfilment to us. The ideal of holiness can no longer be expressed with the reference to the value of nature and thus in opposition to nature and history. The mystic was not against history, but he had to renounce it in various ways because of this opposition.

The consumation of nature removes all mediation between man and God. Thus the post-modern man is brought face to face again with the meaning of Israel. The new *kairos* or time of the Church is the time of fulfilment of nature and history in God, without mediation, typical of the tradition of Israel.

The figure of the Virgin assumed bodily into heaven, which became a solemn dogma in the middle of the twentieth century, is the dominant one in this new period of the Church. Human nature contains the glorious body of Christ and thus the creature in its eschatological fulfilment. Francis' visions ow appears not as crucifixion but as resurrection. Now the fulfilment of nature means nature's own self-government because it has been deified.

It is impossible to describe the new model which is to be formed positively with reference to Mary assumed into heaven, and negatively to Israel of the flesh. Only the Holy Spirit can do this and we cannot pre-empt him. The monastic model implied the renunciation of the political, leaving it to sacral mediation. The martyrdom of Joan of Arc, Savonarola, Thomas More proclaimed the primacy of the person, his or her divine value in the face of every authority, civil or ecclesiastical.[15] But their witness contained a prophetic element of the new *kairos* analogous with Francis' eschatological mysticism. They proclaimed that the city (Florence), the nation (France), all mankind (Utopia) would be transformed into a 'new earth'. To the 'new heaven' of the mystic, the saint of the new *kairos* added the 'new earth' of prophecy, the declaration that human beings and cosmos are present in the eschatology of the Virgin assumed into heaven.

The new model of holiness cannot give up the fruits of the martyrmonastic model, mysticism; it cannot therefore be nothing but political. It must be eschatological. Eschatology opens the silence of the mystic to the word of prophecy.

The new model does not require separation from the world or the conquest of worldly power. It requires the Christian to be present in the world to reveal to it the divine-human fulness of the second coming. The mystic's words of eternal life are coupled with words which recognise the distance that history still has to travel to reach eschatological fulfilment. In the old model the 'political' reached its final expression in the yearning of Thérèsa of Lisieux, it was non-political, and any other word would have been worldly. In the new model the 'political' word is a prophetic word, not like monastic prophecy which pointed out meta-history to history, the future to the present, the individual to the social, but prophecy in the stricter sense which confronts historical limits with the power of Utopia, which carries within the good of the person the good of the community, which already sees history in its eschatological fulfilment.

Separation from history was necessary, it was the figure of the cross. The presence of history is emerging now as the fruit of the cross and the Resurrection. From the first to the second coming, when history comes to an end and all language ceases in the fulness of union.

Translated by Dinah Livingstone

Notes

1. See H. I. Marrou (ed.) *A Diognète* (Sources chrétiennes 33 bis) (Paris 1965).

2. See H. Musurillo (ed.) *The Acts of the Christian Martyrs* (Oxford 1972) pp. 122, 124.

3. *Ibid.* p. 180.

4. C. Leonardi *I Modelli dell' agiografia latina dall'epoca antica al Medioevo, Passagio dal mondo antico al Medioevo: da Teodosio a Gregorio Magno* (Rome, Accademia dei Lincei, due to be published).

5. A. Orbe *Antropologia de san Ireneo* (Madrid 1969); G. Baget-Bozzo *Chiesa e utopia* (Bologna 1971).

6. A. de Vogué 'Monachisme et église dans la pensée de Cassien' *Théologie de la vie monastique* (Paris 1961) pp. 213-240; C. Leonardi 'La conoscenza di Dio in Giovanni Cassiano' *Renovatio* 11 (1976) 53-72.

7. C. Leonardi 'Alle origini della cristianità medievale: Giovanni Cassiano e Salviano di Marsiglia' *Studi Medievali* 18 (1977) 1057-1174.

8. See among others H. Lowe 'Pirmin Willibrord und Bonifatius. Ihre Bedeutung für die Missionsgeschichte ihre Zeit' *La conversione al Cristianesimo dell' Europa dell' Alto Medioevo* (Settimana di studio 14) (Spoleto 1967) pp. 217-261.

9. G. Baget-Bozzo *Cristianesimo e politica, Il partito cristiano al potere* (Florence 1978).

10. F. Graus *Volk, Herrscher und Heiliger im Reich der Merowinger* (Prague 1965); F. Prinz (ed.) *Mönchtum und Gesellschaft im Frünmittelalter* (Darmstadt 1976).

11. G. K. Chesterton *St Francis of Assisi* (London 1932).

12. C. Leonardi 'Storia del Cristo storia del mondo' *Renovatio* 7 (1972) 187-216.

13. G. Baget-Bozzo and C. Leonardi *Il tempo dell' Apocalisse* (Rome 1968); G. Baget-Bozzo 'La fine della cristianità e il comunismo' *Il partito cristiano, il comunismo e la societa radicale* (Florence 1976) pp. 55-107.

14. *Il tempo dell' Apocalisse*. See note 12 above.

15. G. Baget-Bozzo *Chiesa e utopia*. See note 5 above; C. Leonardi 'Tommaso Moro e la figura del vero cristiano' *Renovatio* 9 (1974) 69-75; O. Bucci 'Tommaso Moro: profezia e politica' *ibid.* 220-225.

René Laurentin

Holy Mary

IN THE Church, Mary is holy, the all-holy. She is *panagia,* as the Eastern liturgy puts it with a term that came into use shortly after the Council of Ephesus.

But what kind of holiness is ascribed to Mary, and what is its biblical ground? How has the Church conceived it?

1. A CERTAIN SCRIPTURAL SILENCE

In the sixteenth century Catholics and Protestants implicitly agreed about the 'silence of Scripture' in regard to Mary. The notion would appear justified to some extent as far as the holiness or *sainthood* of Mary is concerned.

The Old Testament does not prophesy the sanctity of the one who would be in travail and bring forth the Messiah (see Micah 5:1-5, a text dependent on Isaiah 7:14 and related to Genesis 3:15 which is a dynastic text).

In the New Testament Mary is not formally qualified as holy. The narratives of the public life do not broach this question. The two logia in which Jesus refers to his mother, that common to the three synoptics— 'Who is my mother?' (Matt. 12:46-50; Mark 3:31-5 and Luke 8:19-21), and that specific to Luke 11:27-8 ('Blessed is the womb that bore you'), carefully refer sanctity to the word of God alone, kept and 'enacted' in accordance with the strict sense of the verb *poiein.* Even John (2:1-12), who allows Mary (among other women, but to the forefront) a positive and dynamic role in the inauguration of Jesus' ministry and at the 'hour' of his death, does not indicate the sanctity of Mary except indirectly, as an intercession which seems to expedite the appearance of the 'hour', and as her availability to the word of the One who avails himself of her readiness, from the cross, for an agonising change of relationship: the mother of Jesus becomes the mother of the type of the disciple.

Whereas the infancy gospel according to Matthew attributes the virginal conception to the action of the Holy Spirit, Mary is treated there only as the object of his action without any indication of her personal sanctity or free participation. Joseph, the male character, is the only active individual in this first infancy gospel. He alone is qualified with praise in the category of sanctity—as a 'just man' (Matt. 1:9).

2. ASPECTS OF MARY'S HOLINESS ACCORDING TO LUKE 1-2

Therefore Luke 1-2 is the only text in the New Testament which reveals the holiness of the mother of the Lord.[1] Gabriel greets her from the start as *Kecharitomonē*. This form of address alliterates (in Greek as well as in the probable Hebrew substrate) with the invitation to Messianic joy: *chaire,* rejoice (1:28). The concept which this signifies is not formally the notion of *sanctity* but that of *grace.* Mary is the object-of-the-gratuitous-favour (*charis*) of God. Gabriel's second annunciation statement is that she has found favour, or grace (1:30).

In the vocational account which comprises the annunciation, this calling has the function of a new name, given to the hero in order to indicate his mission. It is a name given from above, by God. Gideon is greeted thus, as 'mighty man of valour', by the angel of Judges 6:12; as is Cephas, whom Jesus himself calls Peter in Matthew 16:16, and so on. Here the hero is a heroine, her name is an absolute indication of what Luther called *gratia sola*: the preverient initiative of God, its irruption before all merit.

Kecharitomonē is the perfect participle of the very *charitoō*. This grammatical tense connotes a dependable favour: as Osty paraphrases it, 'You who have been and remain the object of favour'. For Mary, everything is grace and has been so since the first moment—as Catholic dogma has it. Luke 1:28, on the other hand, does not formally indicate the fulness which John 1:13 attributes to Christ alone (*plērēs charitos*).

Sanctity is of consequence in this vocation account, which is also a birth narrative. Mary is not castigated in the terms of the vocation of the prophet Hosea who is asked to raise up children to a prostitute—a reference to the lack of faith of Israel—while prophesying that acts of prostitution would be forgotten and that the partner would be received back as a betrothed. Luke places Mary, daughter of Sion, in the condition of the Song of Songs in which the bridegroom can say to his betrothed: 'You are all fair, my love; there is no flaw in you'.

Mary's sanctity is quite gratuitous but not a completed state or something given passively. The annunciation is the proposal of a freedom in which to reflect and deliberate, for freedom is the locus of sanctity. Mary is greatly troubled by the first words of Gabriel and wonders what they mean; Luke 1:29 uses the verb *dialogizeto* (with the same root as 'dialectic' and 'dialogue') to refer to her reflection.

Further on, the dialogue takes shape. Mary asks a question (1:34). She finds enough favour in the eyes of God for her objection, her virginity, to be accepted as legitimate, whereas the parallel objection of Zechariah (1:18) is held against him as lack of faith. In this aspect of the narrative, the parallelism between the two annunciations is paradoxically broken. The priest exercising the supreme function has no right to speak. He is punished in the organ in which he has sinned: 'You will be silent and unable to speak . . . because you did not believe my words' (1:20). Mary, on the contrary, receives a reply which overwhelms her and shows the transcendent nature of her mission. She is to be proclaimed blessed as 'she who believed' (1:45). This contrast reverses another which is less obvious and located at the beginning of the two annunciations. The priest Zechariah is presented as holy: 'righteous before God', but because he is blameless in his observance of all the 'commandments and ordinances of the Lord' (Luke 1:6). On the other hand, the narrator represents Mary without any qualification of her sanctity, as a mere woman (then an inferior state) and, what is more, as a poor young girl from a despised province ('Is the Christ to come from Galilee?' was the appropriate reaction [John 7:41]), and from a despised village: 'Can anything good come out of Nazareth?' (John 1:46). This initial contrast between man and woman, priest and lay-person, sacred and profane, is wholly to the advantage of Zechariah. The glory is on his side and the humble estate on Mary's. But this contrast is reversed by another—that between the law (1:6) and grace (*charis*, 1:28 and 30); hence the daring reversal by Luke of the Pauline adage applied to women: the priest is to be silent in the Church (Zechariah in the Holy of holies), and the woman is to speak and to be glorified by God himself. This is the striking lesson of the contrast between the two annunciations. The Magnificat explains the basic meaning of this revolution in which grace is superior to the law, and the poor are exalted above the rich and powerful.

The reply received by Mary is given formally in terms of holiness. The word 'holy' (*hagios*) recurs twice in Luke 1:35: 'The Holy Spirit will come upon you and the power of the Most High will overshadow you; therefore the child to be born will be called holy, the Son of God'.

This holiness is to be taken in a weighty sense. Luke attributes the birth of the Son of God not only to the Holy Spirit but to the power (*dynamis*) of God, and to the shadow of the *shekina* which formerly covered the ark of the covenant and manifested the presence of God himself. This is signified by the verb *episkiazein,* citing Exodus 40:35 (the occupation of the ark by Yahweh): '. . . the cloud abode upon it and the glory of the

Lord filled the tabernacle.' Luke 1:35 takes up and clarifies this verse. In both, the presence of God is indicated first above the ark and above Mary, the new ark of the covenant, and then within: the glory of God fills the dwelling-place, and Mary receives 'in her womb' (see Luke 1:31), in order to give birth to him, the 'holy one' described as the 'Son of God'.

Mary herself is not directly called holy, but this epithet is used to qualify both the Spirit that comes down upon her[2] and the Holy One who is to be born from her. She is not presented here as an indifferent means or instrument (which is the case in Matthew 1). Instead, she is primarily in a responsive state. 'The Holy Spirit will come upon you, and the power of the Most High will overshadow you.' The pronoun 'you', which refers the gift of God to the individual Mary, seems to operate to the disadvantage of any Christocentrism. While testifying that the Holy Spirit occasions the birth of the Son of God, Luke tends to stress that it is also a matter of a blessing bestowed on Mary, as later on Elizabeth who was 'filled with the Holy Spirit' (Luke 1:41). The two women enter into the circle and efficacy of divine holiness in order to participate in the realisation of the Mystery.

Mary is not therefore a female object, a mere instrument, or an alien body. The convergent allusions in the Old Testament identify her with the Daughter of Sion (the holy people) and with the ark of the covenant (the supreme sacred place),[3] of which she is the eschatological realisation. Hence she becomes (as the Greek homilists were to put it later) a 'living ark'[4]; that is, she is both free and a participant.

And so the account of the annunciation terminates in an explicit, unrestricted act of consent: 'Behold, I am the handmaid of the Lord. Let it be to me according to your word' (Luke 1:38).

The holiness of Mary is that of a servant in accordance with the scriptural tradition derived from second Isaiah, which is to be accomplished in the servant Christ. Later Mary attributes to herself this title of 'servant' (Luke 1:48).

Acquiescing thus (1:38), the mother of the Son of God appears as the one who listens to, keeps, and realises in herself the word of God, in accordance with the essential ideal expressed in the synoptic texts cited above (Luke 8:19-21 and parr; 11:27-8).

Hence the annunciation reconciles the two blessings contrasted in these texts, and with a particular emphasis in Luke 11:27-8: '"Blessed in the womb that bore you, and the breasts that you sucked!" But he said: "Blessed rather are those who hear the word of God and keep it!"'

This union of the two blessings, faith and motherhood, is even more pronounced in the account of the visitation (Luke 1:39-56) whose terminological and structural analogies have been stressed by Raymond Brown. Elizabeth, 'filled with the Holy Spirit', first praises Mary as the 'mother of my Lord' (1:43): 'Blessed are you among women, and blessed is the fruit of your womb!' (1:42).

Mary is blessed (declared to be good: *eulogemenē*). Later she herself recalls this blessing in the Magnificat when she says: '. . . all generations will call be blessed' (*makariousin me*: Luke 1:48). The theocentric interest of our own day is probably surprised that Luke should state the blessedness of Mary before that of Christ. Surely he should have said: 'Blessed is the fruit of your womb, wherefore you are blessed'. But such modern scruples are alien to Luke and to his literary source, in this case Judith 13:18: '. . . you are blessed by the Most High God above all women on earth; and blessed be the Lord God . . .'

The blessing of Mary as mother passes into the blessing for faith: 'And blessed is she who believed that there would be a fulfilment of what was spoken to her from the Lord'.

In the Magnificat, Mary refers her blessing and her happiness to the grace of God alone who has regarded the *tapeinosis* (poverty, humility, lowliness) of his handmaiden (1:48). In her exaltation and in her exultation in the One whose name is holy (Luke 1:43; see 1:35), she perceives the type of the exaltation of the poor by means of that divine revolution which is the theme of the Magnificat. This hymn, which some commentators have tried to interpret as an erratic fragment, is therefore a lyrical expression well integrated into Luke 1 (in significance and terminology), and also one that fits the Old Testament admirably (without anachronism).

The holiness of Mary is recalled in more discreet terms in the account of the nativity (Luke 2:1-19). There she appears as a sign among others of the coming of the Lord of glory (2:11) in the form of a child: the manger and the swaddling-clothes in which Mary herself has wrapped the infant (2:7, 12, 16—three verses, for Luke stresses the point). But he does not omit the inward activity in which real sanctity is to be found, according to the gospel. The pericope terminates in these words: 'But Mary kept all these things (*rēmata*), pondering them in her heart' (2:19).

The word *rēmata* means literally 'words', but in the acceptation of the Hebrew word *dabar* which designates not only words but the events which they signify. Mary does not keep them passively but actively. She confronts these *rēmata* (that is, the events and the scriptures which foretell them) in accordance with the continuing process of Luke 1:2. This active meditation on Mary's part is expressed by the participle *symballousa,* which means the conjunction and confrontation of these word-events. It is no accident that the word *symballousa* should have the same root as the word 'symbol'. It is a symbolic meditation. It is a meditation on signs in order to discern their import. Later, Luke returns to this meditation of Mary's at the end of the infancy narrative, without

reusing the word *symballousa,* though he does universalise the reference
of the meditation: Mary stored up all these things (*rēmata*) in her heart.

Further aspects of Mary's holiness are revealed in the last two episodes
of the infancy narrative:

1. She is engaged in observance of the 'law of Moses' which is mentioned three times in Luke 2:22-4. Although Mary's holiness has been
characterised by the use of 'grace' (in contrast with Zachary's and Anne's,
which is *only* in accordance with the law), she is not without the law,
which grace does not exclude but accomplishes.

2. This holiness is prophetically connected with the suffering that will
be experienced by the Messiah who is raised up as a sign of contradiction
(2:35). This is a mysterious and incomprehensible suffering which Mary
will not 'understand' directly (Luke 2:50). This prophecy is realised
initially in a prophetic and symbolic form in the childhood of Christ. He
disappears, to his mother's distress (2:48), at Jerusalem, at the feast of the
Passover, for three days under conditions which predict his death in the
very same city, at the time of the very same feast, when he will return to
his Father (Luke 2:49 and 23:46).[5] This requires Mary to begin a new
phase of meditation in the darkness inherent in faith (Luke 1:45 and
2:50).

3. GENERAL VIEW OF THE TRADITION

The holiness of Mary insisted on by Luke has been variously explained
in different ages and cultures.

In the second century environment, the proto-gospel of James found it
necessary to say something more about Mary's sanctity. It did so under
the pressure of a lively, naïve and imaginative popular enthusiasm, but in
accordance with the schemata of Judaeo-Christian ritual holiness, by
referring to legal purity and impurity. According to this narrative, Mary
was conceived when her father Joachim was at prayer and away from his
wife. Her mother nevertheless thought of herself as insufficiently pure
and did not breast-feed her child until after forty days of ritual purifi-
cation. She took care that the feet of the child Mary should not touch the
ground until the moment when she was placed on the sacred steps of the
Temple. She was then to reside in the Holy of holies and to be fed by
angels.[6]

Other texts from the early Christian period also look back to Luke.
They are restricted to an external, objective consideration of the holiness
of Mary in the style of Matthew. The Virgin is then a sign of mystery.
There is no emphasis on her personal, active and inward sanctity. The
Fathers of the Church, from Origen to Chrysostom and Cyril of Alex-
andria, allowed themselves to be carried along by verbal liberality and

paraenetic speculation, to such an extent even that they discerned in Mary suggestions of vainglory (at Cana, John 2), or of doubt (at the cross, John 19:25-7). Simeon's sword, exposing (adverse) thought in the depths of human hearts (Luke 2:35), would be the appropriate symbol in this case.[7] These paradoxical, superficial reflections may be traced to the orator's urge to shock by touching on a sensitive point of Christian tradition which already offered an elevated conception of Mary. These negative themes were to disappear in the West with Ambrose and Augustine, and somewhat later in the East, not without a strange recurrence in an isolated twelfth century text recently analysed by G. Jouassard.[8]

It was the development of the ascetic life and especially of virginal sisterhoods that focused attention on Mary's holiness. Athanasius[9] and Ambrose[10] (who paraphrases Athanasius) represent Mary to consecrated virgins as a model whose favourable attitudes they express in concrete form: she is modest, discreet, and unacquainted with public places (p. 60); but they do not have recourse to the spiritual inspiration of Luke. Mary is made to appear as a model of the hidden life, but the dynamism of the annunciation and above all the revolutionary inspiration of the Magnificat are not mentioned.

From the fifth century, the Greeks gradually came to acknowledge the complete holiness and purity of the Theotokos, who was more elevated than the angels, cherubim and seraphim. The homilists identified her symbolically with all the sacred temple objects.[11] But this was an overall, objective consideration. They more rarely expressed the inward freedom so firmly stressed by Luke. They exalted instead the sanctity of the Theotokos, not without some obfuscation of the synoptic texts in which the Lord challenged praise grounded on nothing more than Mary's motherhood (Luke 11:28). At the high point of this development, Mariology (in contrast to the so-called anti-Mariological gospel texts) established as a thesis the point that Mary's motherhood was superior to her fulness of grace and to her theological life.

The pseudo-Albert (in the middle of the thirteenth century) exposed all the details of this fulness. He conceived the fulness of grace as a form of omnicompetence comprising all possible virtues, gifts and charisms, right up to speaking in tongues and interpretation. He examines all this minutely in nearly two hundred chapters.[12]

There have been quite diverse tendencies in this regard in modern times. The Mariology of the seventeenth to twentieth centuries, up to Pius XII, exalted Mary's sanctity with a strong trend towards assimilation to Christ, in accordance with the law of 'homonymy' already followed by the Greek homilists. This resulted in constructions that were often artificial. Yet Thérèsa of Lisieux[13] reacted against them and once again brought out the humble, forceful essence of the simple but imitable Mary, in the sense of Luke 1. After Pius XII, the process of stripping down the Marian image continued; this was sometimes radical in nature and not without a certain reductive effect. In contemporary catechetics Mary is frequently an uninspiring figure. She appears as 'the mother of Jesus' or 'Joseph's wife'. It seems appropriate to be reticent about the 'Virgin Mary'. Jesus has a father and a mother like the little boys and little girls in the RE books—no more and no less. Mary is a rather commonplace silhouette without any spiritual features. The dogma of her holiness is hardly taught in modern catechesis. In the course of history Mary's sanctity has been invoked in terms of legitimately diverse cultural suasions, but with unfortunate swings between supererogation and reductivism. These two abuses of excess and neglect both forget the essential aspect of Mary. However noble the expressions of the understanding of Mary over nineteen centuries may sometimes be, in the end we are referred to the incomparable richness of Luke 1-2. According to Luke, Mary is not only the mother of the Lord who is the Son of God, and his eschatological sanctuary, the new ark of the convenant sanctified by the Holy Spirit, but the prototype of a free, active holiness overflowing with charisma—above all that prophecy which shines out in the Magnificat and the bountiful outpouring of Pentecost (Acts 1:14 and 2:1-12). Her vocation is to shape the body of Christ and to be its prime sanctuary, and thus to be an example for all those who share in it.

Translated by John Cumming

Notes

1. An artificially systematic practice of historico-critical methodology has sometimes caused the infancy narratives to be thoutht of as a late and synthetic fabrication. A methodical evaluation of the text, such as has been carried out several times since 1956 (R. Laurentin *Structure et théologie de Luc* [Paris 1956]) seems to me to show that these two chapters are an (in several respects archaic) expression of the Judaeo-Christian community in which Mary lived and articulated herself. Otherwise it would seem difficult to explain the inspiration and extraordinary consistency of these texts, which continually offer new enlightenment in response to the efforts of new methodology applied in a non-reductive spirit. This is not a matter of literary construction as exegetes sometimes conceive it when they are neither writers nor inspired.

2. I refer here to the substantial doctrine of the Old Testament on the holiness of God and his spirit of holiness who is the spirit of sanctification. One of these culminating points is Ezekiel 36-8.

3. R. Laurentin *Structure et théologie de Luc 1-2* (Paris 1956). This work is a methodical study of the allusions of Luke 1-2 to the Old Testament. These

convergent scriptural allusions and recurrences tend to identify the Son of Mary not only with the Messiah but with the Lord God himself, and Mary with the eschatological Daughter of Sion (Zephaniah 3) and with the ark of the convenant (Luke 1:35 and 40:35; Luke 1:39-56 and 2 Samuel 6).

4. On this qualification often met with among the Greek homilists, see R. Laurentin *Marie, l'Eglise et le sacerdoce* (Paris 1952) p. 78, n. 18, n. 10 and p. 82.

5. R. Laurentin *Jésus et le Temple* (Paris 1966) establishes the references of Luke 2:40-52 to the passion. The episode of the finding in the temple, a typically Lukan conclusion of the infancy narrative, intentionally anticipates the themes that will conclude the entire gospel.

6. E. de Strycker *La forme la plus ancienne du Protoévangile de Jacques* (Brussels 1961) pp. 81-101 (4:2 to 8:1).

7. G. Jouassard 'Le problème de la sainteté de Marie chez les Pères depuis les origines de la patristique jusqu'au Concile d'Ephèse' in *Etudes mariales* 5, (1947) 13-31; and various further studies, especially in H. du Manoir *Maria* 1, and so on.

8. G. Jouassard 'Un témoignage inattendu du XIIe siècle sur la doctrine mariale' in *Revue d'études augustiniennes* 21 (1975) 197-201. This anonymous twelfth-century text seems to ignore the maxim universally accepted since Augustine which said that 'there can be no question of sin when Mary is in question' (*De natura et gratia*, PL 44 267; CSEL 60, 263-4). The anonymous author in fact accords it this restriction: *licet ante conceptionem Verbi quodlibet veniale forsitan habuisset* (Serm. 13 of MS Lincoln 201, published in *Sacris Erudiri* 15 (1964) 70.

9. The text of Athanasius discovered in a Coptic version was published by L. T. Lefort 'Athanase . . . sur la virginité' in *Le Museon* 48 (1935) 55-73.

10. Ambrose *De virginibus ad Marcellinam* liber 2, c. 2-3, Nos. 6-19, PL 16, 208B-211C, ed. O. Faller *Florilegium patristicum* pp. 47-52.

11. R. Laurentin *Marie, l'Eglise et le sacerdoce* (Paris 1952) pp. 57-61 and 76-85.

12. *Mariale,* published among the works of Albertus Magnus, vol. 37 of the standard French editor. On the question of omnicompetence which dominates the interpretation of pseudo-Albert, see R. Laurentin *Marie, l'Eglise et le sacerdoce* (Paris 1952) pp. 185-186. The author describes in detail, one after the other, all the virtues (questions 44-61), the gifts (62-69), the blessings (70-77), the halos (79-80), fruits (81-94), the graces *gratis datae* (95-122), the special and singular graces (124-150), the characteristics of the nine choirs of angels (150-161), and the benedictions of the twelve patriarchs (170-193).

13. Thérèsa of Lisieux reacted above all in her canticle *Pourquoi j'aime Marie* (May 1897). The theme is that the motive for loving Mary is not false elevation or exceptional privileges that would remove one from the ordinary condition: 'Ravishings, miracles, ecstasies' (stanza 17), but having lived and suffered simply, like us 'in the dark night of faith' (R. Laurentin, *Thérèsa of Lisieux,* [Paris 1973] pp. 172-174).

Christian Duquoc

The Holiness of Jesus and the Holiness of the Spirit

'WHICH OF you convicts me of sin?' Christ replied to his opponents (John 8:46). The fact that one cannot be accused of sin is a recognition of holiness. Jesus lived in harmony with God his Father and carried out the Father's will. At the same time, however, it cannot be denied that a number of questions are raised by formulae of this kind when they are divorced from their context in the gospel narrative.

There is ample evidence of the fluid nature of this idea in the history of Christian sanctity as revealed in various processes of canonisation. In saying that Jesus is holy, we are at once running the risk of attributing to him certain tendentious images that we have ourselves elaborated. We respond, for example, to the evangelical counsel: 'You must be perfect, as your heavenly Father is perfect' (Matt. 5:48) by practices of perfection which are often only partially derived from the gospel. Our representations of Jesus too are as varied as our models of holiness. In the popular tradition of spirituality, the notion of what constitutes sanctity has always been subject to many changes, no doubt because of most people's tendency to eliminate the historical figure of Jesus in considering holiness. The imagination is left free to construct a model in accordance with individual or collective wishes. But if we are to speak about the holiness of Jesus, we are bound to go back to his history.

In the first place, Jesus is remote from us in time. The gospel texts which bear witness to his activity and preaching have been subjected to many different interpretations, discussions and selections, all of which form part of the life and work of groups of readers, professional and non-professional, of the New Testament.

Giving a contemporary interpretation to the gospel consists in choosing from Scripture what the Christian community at that particular time believes to be suitable to the period. This selection therefore implies an exclusion. Imagining the holiness of Jesus as being at the service of what society today expects from that holiness is therefore a judgement of the authenticity of that holiness on the basis of contemporary standards. A person is only regarded as holy if his activity is believed to have a holy effect on society. The figure of Jesus of Nazareth cannot be entirely exempted from these demands. Hypothetically at least, we may, however, hope that our contemporary reconstruction will contain some of the impetus of his original holiness. The contemporary interpretation is not, after all, left completely to the arbitrary nature of our imagination, since the Spirit, who calls Jesus to mind, gives him a contemporary image for us. We may therefore conclude that there are two factors which come together in forming our judgement of Jesus' holiness. The first is his historical activity as recorded in the gospels and the second is the witness borne by the Spirit, a witness that is always contemporary.

Jesus is not a myth of innocence and holiness. He was the subject of an action that led to his death. I do not have to describe that action here, but will assume that it is well known. The prophet of Nazareth took up a position within the Jewish religion that gave rise to defensive attitude on the part of the protagonists of Judaism. They thought that his activity was strenuously opposed to the tradition that they venerated because it had come from Moses. Jesus was, in other words, not holy in the sense in which the most religious and zealous people among his listeners conceived holiness.

The authors of both the synoptic and the fourth gospels were opposed to this interpretation of Jesus' activity and preaching. For them, he was not the blasphemer and imposter that his opponents accused him of being. His justification by God at Easter testified to his holiness. God had made the path followed by Jesus his own by raising him from the dead. This was an objective confession of faith, which had nothing to say about the way in which Jesus subjectively carried out his mission or was related to God. The spiritual struggles which Jesus may well have undergone are assessed very soberly in Scripture.

We may briefly consider some scriptural examples of what might be termed Jesus' holiness. There is his jubilation about the revelation of the good news to the little ones (Matt. 11:25-28) and the various pronouncements gathered together in the Sermon on the Mount are, I think, inspired by Jesus' own concrete choices and are not theoretical considerations, but true expressions of his own activity. He was also not trying to construct a utopia, but describing what he himself put into practice in his own life and death when he insisted that love of one's enemies was an essential characteristic of his disciples (Matt. 5:38-48). Jesus did not have enemies and in so doing he created enemies for himself. He did not, however, share in their reasoning and, when they had him put to death, he did not curse them, but forgave them. He was able to demand from his disciples the same excess of forgiveness ('seventy times seven', Matt. 18:22) that he himself had given. This excess provides, in my opinion, a good objective criterion of his holiness.

Jesus did not name an enemy or a scapegoat who would explain the wretched situation in which his people were placed or the bad relationship existing between God and men. He did not take part in the Messianic violence which was so prevalent at the time in which he was living and which had led to the unfounded conviction that pagans and faithless Jews were soon to be destroyed. He did not believe that the kingdom of God would be closed to those who were considered by men to be unworthy to enter it. He even claimed that he had not come to save the just.

Like the Pharisee in the parable (Luke 18:9-15), these just Jews were more concerned to distinguish themselves from sinners than to practise in their lives the justice that was pleasing to God. They were not like the sinners. They belonged to the chosen people and were by nature on the side of good. Because of this, they defended themselves strenuously against anything and anyone who might violate their privileged position. God was with them because they were with God and their cause and the cause of right were the same.

Jesus, on the other hand, did not try to distinguish himself from anyone. He ate both with sinners and with the Pharisees. He was also no less strenuous in denouncing the destructive effects of religious patriotism, which consigned to despairing oblivion all those who lacked either the opportunity or the power to share in this privilege. Those who lacked the opportunity were the pagans, who were excluded because they had not been chosen. Their very birth condemned them to life outisde the kingdom. Those who lacked the power were the faithless Jews who had not been able to study or practise the law. Jesus was not concerned with opportunity or power in this context; he was only conscious of the need for all people, from the east and the west, to share in the feast of the kingdom of God. He described how quickly the poor and the crippled entered the hall and how disdainfully those who had been invited reacted. They—the just Jews—did not risk their reputation by associating with those who lacked opportunity or power. They preferred not to take up their places and, by excluding sinners, they exiled themselves from the feast.

The quality and the direction of Jesus' holiness is clear from these and other choices. He is perfect as his heavenly Father is perfect, the Father 'who makes his sun rise on the evil and on the good' (Matt. 5:25). Paradoxically, Jesus did not at first oppose the evil or those who were considered to be evil—he was opposed to good men who reduced the evil to the level of evil and condemned them to despair. It is precisely this orientation that accounts for the distance placed between himself and the law and the new form of exclusion that produced his holiness.

He was in no sense a zealot with regard to the law. This is clearly illustrated in the story of the woman taken in adultery (John 8:3-11). It hardly matters whether this was or was not historical. If it was in fact a creation on the part of the early Christian community, it would bear witness to the very early idea that the first Christians had of Jesus' freedom and holiness.

The story tells us that the woman had committed a serious breach of the law. She had damaged the community's self-respect by not carrying out the demands made by the covenant in her behaviour. For this reason, she had to be excluded from the community; the penalty for her offence was death.

Those who accused her, the zealots of the law, confronted Jesus with a serious difficulty. On the one hand, he could resist the carrying out of the law and thereby introduce a form of permissiveness which would, in the long run, lead to the community's losing its identity, because, if the law was less rigorous on its application, the differences between the people of Israel and the pagans would eventually be obscured. On the other hand, however, he could uphold the law and its implementation, in which case he would be going back on his own judgement and contradicting his previous behaviour with regard to sinners and those who were excluded from the community, such as tax-collectors and prostitutes. A rigorous interpretation of the law would reduce the scope of his message about the breakthrough of the kingdom of God. Jesus had, after all, come to proclaim a time of grace, not a time of judgement and condemnation.

Jesus in fact avoided both horns of the dilemma. He did not take up the position of one who was zealous for the law, since this would have been contrary to the direction of his prophetic work, which consisted in not judging and in coming closer to those who were at a distance. On the other hand, however, he did not advocate breaking the law if this did not have the aim of making hope rise again or pointing to forgiveness. He therefore turned the problem back again on to his questioners, who set themselves up as accusers, aggressively attacking a young Israelite woman in the name of their zeal for the law. He clearly wanted their aggression to be logical to its ultimate conclusion. If they were not guilty of any debt to the law, they could be both accusers and judges. In this way, Jesus unmasked the objectivity of the law, insisting that the accuser should not be in a position were he could himself be accused. The aggression that he uses against others should not in any case be used against himself. What Jesus was, in other words, saying was that only an innocent man can be a judge.

Having turned the zealots' aggression back on themselves, Jesus was left alone with the woman. He who was innocent did not condemn her. His attitude in this story is clearly an indication of the pattern of his holiness. He rejects scepticism that might lead to permissiveness on the one hand and, on the other, a condemnation that might favour sectarianism and a wrongly based clear conscience. Above all, his attitude draws attention to the fact that the law fails to achieve its aim if it leads to despair, in other words, if it commits people to exclusion.

Another aspect of Jesus' holiness, his concern that the kingdom of God should not be treated like a family possession, is stressed in the parable of the prodigal son (Luke 15:11-32). One very common interpretation of this parable places the emphasis on the goodness of the father. The mercy which the father shows to the son who has left his house after having demanded the inheritance which was his by right is, in this interpretation, greatly stressed. This is a valid interpretation, but the parable can also equally well be interpreted if the humble attitude of the prodigal son is given central importance. Neither of these two interpretations, however, seem to me to be faithful to the original purport of the parable, which is the conflict between the just and faithful older son and the younger son who is in flight.

The father suggests that the just and faithful son should be in the real sense a brother to the son who has run away and asks him not to make his sense of justice and his faithfulness the reason for opposing his brother. He implores him to be happy that he has a brother, whatever that brother may have done. The older brother would follow the natural tendency of justice and exclude the younger brother. The obvious merit of his action cannot be disputed. It is clear, however, that it is not the sinful younger brother who refuses to accept the idea of authentic brotherhood, but the just older brother.

Jesus is the just and faithful son, but, far from following the inherent logic of the law as the older brother in the parable did, he becomes in a very real way the brother of those who are excluded. He does not make a victim of his innocence, nor does he make his right as the first-born an exclusive possession. Without any reservation, he is ready to share with others the good fortune that is his by right. His justice and his faithfulness are very different from those of the older son in the parable.

The original orientation of Jesus' holiness would seem to be characterised by the desire, which is made objective and concrete in his actions and his preaching, not to have enemies. He did not accept the logic of the social law, according to which the solidarity of the group is strengthened by the creation of an enemy or a scapegoat. It may be thought that this idea is unrealistic and that it has been disproved again and again in the history of Christianity. On the other hand, it may also be thought that this point of view is eminently realistic and that Christianity has survived for so many centuries precisely because it has again and again questioned its instinctive group behaviour, that is, the need to create an enemy in order to define its identity and be assured of the solidarity of the group. I am inclined to think that the early Church, following Jesus, had a therapeutic reason for attributing hostile behaviour to spiritual powers in general and Satan in particular. Christians, the early believers thought, did not have enemies in this world, because their world was not on earth. Christians could therefore be brothers in the full sense of the word because no race of men and no class of human being had been designated as an enemy by Jesus Christ.

Paradoxically, it was because he behaved in this way that he himself made enemies. At the same time, however, he always forgave those who hated him, hoping in this way that they would not cling to an identity based on the exclusion of the man who was different.

If this anyalsis is correct and relevant to the case, it clearly shows that Jesus' holiness was not a form of purity, in the sense of a separation from whatever was likely to do harm to the image that we like to bestow on ourselves. On the contrary, it consisted in forgiving all those who were his enemies. This attitude formed a practical basis for his Sermon on the Mount and in particular for his declaration that the 'meek' were blessed and for his commandment to love one's enemies.

Although the descriptions of Jesus' holiness found in the classical theology of the Church are not without interest, they are undoubtedly too abstract and tend to hand on a previously established image of the holiness of God, thus overlooking the concrete way in which Jesus lived. The action of the Spirit, who is traditionally described as holy, can also be seen as taking place within the framework of this holy attitude which gives hope to those who are without hope.

The function of the Spirit cannot be separated from the words and actions of Jesus in the Christian tradition. This does not mean that the Spirit does not act outside the Church's sphere of influence. What it means is that, within Christianity, the Spirit above all has the function of calling Jesus to mind and it is this function that forms the pivot around which all interpretation turns.

The Spirit enables us to remember Jesus during the interim period because it is the source of the Church's activity and preaching. Jesus claimed to act in the Spirit, saying that the man who attributed his activity to the work of demons was 'blaspheming against the Holy Spirit' (Mark 3:29).

There is, then, a continuity between the actions, the words and the function of the Spirit and those of Jesus. The Spirit, given to Christians by the risen Christ to make them holy has a function that is analogous to that of Jesus. 'From his mouth issued a sharp two-edged sword' (Apoc. 1:16): Jesus' prophetic words can be compared to a sword that separates. They have the effect of a judgement or a decision and are similar in effect to a process of exclusion and are therefore apparently contradictory to what we have already said above about Jesus' attitude.

It would, however, be wrong to base the effect of Jesus' prophetic words on an image of separation or exclusion. His words certainly do separate, but they separate because they are creative. All birth is a form of separation, since coming into the world is breaking with the previous state of being. The child leaves the warm, enclosed womb and enters an open space. The act by which a human being inaugurates an autonomous life is an act of separation. 'He has not yet broken the umbilical cord' we say of someone who has not achieved full freedom. Jesus' prophetic words open up a new space, cut the umbilical cord and take us away from the maternal religion. They are in this sense a form of separation brought about by the action of the Spirit.

The Spirit, then, is holy because he separates. This, however, is an ambiguous statement. The Pharisees called themselves those who were separated. The Essenes also tended to achieve purity by separating themselves from everything that they regarded as impure. Many Israelites were very conscious of the principle stated in the book of Leviticus: 'You shall be holy, for I, the Lord your God, am holy' (Lev. 19:2) and as a result separated themselves, if not externally from the mass of the people, then at least inwardly, by a practice that was so exceptional that they became effectively cut off.

Those who had opted to follow the law rigorously were able, by organising their life within a legal network that separated them from the pagans and from sinners and those who were in one way or another impure, to live in a holy space in which they could be free of possible harm to themselves and be fully conscious of their privileged position. This form of separation was sometimes obsessive—for example, nothing that was unclean was allowed to touch the one who was separated, so that he could remain in the state of purity that was assured by the practice of the law. The law therefore set part of the population on one side, alerting these separated people to the dangers of associating with others and accepting any novelty. It enclosed them within a sphere that they hoped was completely closed.

The Spirit also separates, but in quite a different way. The separation of the Spirit is rather a kind of transgression. He questions and allows doubt to enter the minds of men. In the New Testament, certain figures are presented as adversaries of Jesus. The adversary who corresponds most closely in function to the Holy Spirit is Beelzebub, a figure pointing to the fact that separation for the sake of purity is against the will of God. This form of separation is not creative. It is not in accordance with the spirit of the exodus. It is not, in a word, open to the future.

In his relationship with Jesus, as recorded in the New Testament, the Spirit undoubtedly forms part of this movement towards the future. This is vividly illustrated in the account of the annunciation (Luke 1:26-39). The experience of Easter formed the basis of this story. Various opposing factors intersect within the account, the most important being the people's Messianic hope and their bitter disappointment over Jesus' death on Good Friday, pointing to the apparent failure of his mission. The opposition between these two elements underlies the whole account of the annunciation. The one who was called Lord, Messiah and Son did not acquire these titles in continuity with the hope that men had experienced previously—he was proclaimed Lord on the basis of a radical break or separation, that of death. The earlier hope was therefore changed by this experience. The Spirit, we may therefore say, is creative because he separates men from their earlier, Davidic expectations of a Messiah and takes them into a different sphere, that of the living Son and Lord. We can, in other words, confess Christ to be Lord only on the basis of his future, not on the basis of his past. He cannot be identified, from the time of his death and resurrection onwards, as the Son of David. The earlier assurances are of no value in so far as they are not open to the future.

This process can be ascertained in the story of the temptation in the desert (Luke 4:1-14) as well as in the example given above. The Spirit is said to have driven Jesus out into the desert, where he was put to the test. This test is fundamentally one in which Jesus does not let himself be led astray by immediate satisfaction—the satisfaction of abundance, prestige and power. In this case, however, it was not simply a question of working for his own profit. What was involved was the future of the people who were above all influenced by the Messianic expectations that were current at the time of Jesus. The satisfaction of abundance, prestige and power was not in itself perverse, but, presented as Messianic consequences and indeed as divine effects, these three forms of immediate satisfaction made

God the servant of men's desires, enclosing him within the limitations of a closed space. The Spirit does not, on the contrary, enclose man within his immediate satisfaction, but leads him into the desert. The prophetic words of Jesus have their origin in this open space.

Jesus' preaching and his miracles also took place within this open space. The cure of the woman who had been ill for eighteen years (Luke 13:10-18) is a good example of this. Jesus healed her on the sabbath, the day that was dedicated to the honour of God. The leader of the synagogue told the people that, since God did not work on the sabbath, it was surely possible for all necessary cures to be carried out on the six working days.

Jesus did not see the matter in this light. If the sabbath was a day that was dedicated to God, he believed, it should also be a day on which men could be free. This woman had been ill for eighteen years. She recognised that Jesus was a prophet who could put an end to her suffering. It would have been quite wrong to send her away, urging her to be patient until the next day. It was not possible to disturb God in any way on the sabbath. He was concerned with his glory and was not interested in the cure of a sick woman.

Jesus, however, recognised that God's glory consisted in this woman being made free. Neither the sabbath nor the law have any positive meaning if all that they do is to enslave men. The God who is honoured in this way cannot be God and he would ignore his day of rest and his glory if they had destructive effect. Jesus' action was therefore in accordance with the activity of the Spirit—he separated the insistence on carrying out the law that was imposed on God in the name of his so-called honour. God is as unpredictable as his Spirit and cannot be enclosed within the demands made by a religious system.

The similarity between the holiness of the Spirit and Jesus' activity is perhaps even more clearly illustrated in the resurrection. The idea of resurrection is today open to doubt rather than to belief. It is often attributed to a desire to escape from the finite nature of death or to experience death as a return to the womb and a state of rest. The idea of resurrection is seen as expressing our inability to live here and now in the world as it is and our need to dream of a life which is in no sense differentiated and is nothing other than death.

It would be foolish to deny that many Christians have this desire, but it would be equally wrong not to recognise a symbolic logic in Christianity. The resurrection is not an isolated idea, independent of the whole Christian movement. Within this whole, the resurrection takes place on the basis of a separation—Jesus risked his life rather than give way to the popular desires which might have made him successful. He was able to perceive, under the threat of death, what was significant for the future. All the other Messianic figures were forgotten, but the way opened by

Jesus has lasted, since he faced death in the hope, not of a return to paradise, but of a new creation. He did not give way to a nostalgia for the past, a desire that was all too evident in the immediate hopes of those who followed him. Because he was able, in the hope that he placed in God, to continue on his path as far as death, he became the giver of the Spirit.

It is not possible to define in advance the conditions governing holiness. It does not consist in conforming to a law or infallibly obeying a rule of life. Jesus' holiness, which is given a contemporary value as a dynamic principle by the present gift of the Spirit, cannot be classed as a model. None of us could reproduce it in all its aspects, express it as a universal rule or find strict terms in order to define it.

Despite the ambiguity of the image, I have described Jesus' holiness as having the function of separating. This does not mean that Jesus separated himself from the world or became an ascetic in an élitist sense. He did not, in other words, follow the path of John the Baptist. Nor did he form a sect. On the contrary, he called all men to the feast of the kingdom, even though he did not impose a rule of life. Those who enter the kingdom are those who forgive seventy times seven, who do not separate themselves from their brothers and who do not make enemies. There are no real rules for these limits and the disciple of Jesus is creative. It is in this sense that the holiness of Jesus is to be found in the framework opened by the activity of the Spirit—because his holiness has a creative and separating function which allows us to call on God the Father and to do his will.

To do the Father's will seems to have been the mainspring of all Jesus' activity. He was obedient to death and his freedom was made manifest in that obedience. It would be a misunderstanding of his statement: 'You must be perfect, as your heavenly Father is perfect' if we were to interpret this injunction to do the Father's will as a previously existing commandment to be carried out by Jesus himself. The will of the Father 'makes his sun rise on the evil and on the good' and this can be called a kind of anti-narcissism. It is not that men should not have self-respect or should not love themselves—these are the measure of men's love for others. What anti-narcissism really means here is that we should not be closed to the possibilities that are opened to us by God's freedom and love. God overcomes the fascination that we have for the past by making us enter an unsuspected future.

For Jesus, then, doing God's will was being free to perceive the objective situation. Jesus was neither afraid nor distressed and it may be this freedom from fear and distress that makes him seem to us to be a holy figure. He was quite clear about what was involved in his activity and the fact that it might result in his being condemned, yet he continued to work for the establishment of a space of hope, without ever calling on God to intervene. Scripture bears ample witness to the clarity and the serenity of Jesus.

He was holy because he allowed the creative Spirit to work within him, separating the norms imposed by the past. He boldly entered a new creation, although its form was beyond suspicion and the way towards it led to death.

Translated by David Smith

Part II

Bulletins

Joseph Spae

Buddhist Models of Holiness

AT FIRST Christian blush, Buddhism appears as a vat of contradictions: doctrinally, it denies the existence of a personal God and yet, existentially, it affirms man's capacity to meet and imitate superhuman saints and saviours. It denies the existence of an immortal soul, and yet it accepts man's personal continuity in a multitude of rebirths until liberation or enlightenment is reached. These contradictions, to Buddhists, are only apparent and marginal.

Amidst a variety of sects and doctrines, Buddhists hold that it is the historical Siddharta Gautama, the Buddha, who proclaimed the supreme and definitive goal of sanctity during the forty-five years of his earthly ministry which started c. 530 B.C. with his celebrated first sermon near Benares. This sermon addresses itself to the individual and enjoins him to lead a life of perfection. Indeed, holiness is the heart of Buddhism. It manifests itself at several levels. Doctrinally, the Buddha described it in the Four Holy Truths: Life is fraught with suffering; the source of all suffering is the craving for sensual pleasures, for an afterlife, or for annihilation; there is a way out of that suffering through the cessation of craving; and there is a final state of bliss and perfection which is nirvana. The modalities of a life of holiness are put in practice along the Holy Eightfold Path, a vigorous Middle Way between vulgar pleasure-seeking and futile asceticism. This style of life which leads safely to enlightenment consists of the following: saintly views and intentions, which is a matter of faith and rests on the charism of wisdom; saintly speech, action and livelihood, which belong to the realm of morality; saintly efforts, mindfulness and mental concentration, which are the domain of meditation and put the crown on the spiritual life.

The perception of the Four Holy Truths and the practice of the Holy Eightfold Path are not, as such, separate stages of spiritual growth.

Buddhist sanctity is holistic, synchronic, affective and intuitive. In theological terms one might say that it is both a grace and an effort, a task and a responsibility. One classic text in which the Buddha describes this new world of spiritual totality is this: 'Great is the advantage of meditation steeped in morality, and great is the advantage of wisdom steeped in meditation.' (*Mahāparinibbānasutta,* 1:12) Buddhists, then, are familiar with heroes of sanctity, and they feel close to them as exemplars, guides, and saviours.

1. THE BUDDHA, PARAGON OF SANCTITY

The Buddha (*c.* 560-480 B.C.) experienced total awakening, hence his name. He was endowed with tremendous personal charm and charity, no doubt considerably embellished by later ages but still powerful enough to attract millions of people. The holiness which he preached is an inner call for happiness. He taught that there is no opposition between man and the rest of the sentient world because all join in the spiritualisation of all that exists through consciousness of the Ultimate Reality. Buddhist perfection, again in Western terms, is at the same time theistic, atheistic and pantheistic, monistic and dualistic, personal and impersonal, esoteric and exoteric. Perfection is a matter of man's total being seen as one of the many perfectible stages of life.

The historical Buddha never claimed to be the ultimate source of holiness, as God is for Christians. He is not the Way, even though he points to it. Hence, the Buddhist saint does not 'participate' in the Buddha's life but rather realises himself through the practice of virtues. The Buddha's inner-worldly compassion is the saint's standard of perfection; it is detachment from the world for the sake of the salvation of the world. Sanctity is total liberation from the endless cycles of life-and-death, *karma,* from the shackles of self; it means that endless bliss which is nirvana.

Of great importance are the Buddha's precepts and exhortations still observed today. Buddhists, monks and laity alike, pledge themselves to observe five basic precepts: not taking life, not using what is not given, not engaging in illicit sex, not telling lies, and not drinking liquor. The code for monks and nuns is much more detailed and runs in the hundreds of precepts the observance of which sets the pace of one's spiritual life. Progress calls for the use of spiritual techniques, mainly of meditation. This illustrates the unity of the spiritual life, and the need for interiority which leads to freedom from sensual desires, i.e., from the causes of sin. He who conquers these causes or, in other words, belief in a separate self which accounts for suffering and rebirth, is on the point of becoming a saint.

2. A TYPOLOGY OF BUDDHIST SANCTITY

Buddhism sets forth a series of stages along the path to holiness. From low to high there are four categories of saints according to Theravada texts: 1. The stream-winner, *sotapanna,* who will no longer be reborn in hell, as an animal, or in any state of suffering because he has destroyed the first three of ten obstacles to sanctity, from reliance on good works to ignorance about the self. 2. The once-returner, *sakadagamin,* who conquered also lust and hate, and shall be reborn only once. 3. The non-returner, *anagamin,* who will be reborn in the higher heavens and thence reach nirvana. 4. Finally, the *arhat* or 'worthy one', who completes the course of salvation at the end of this life.

It has often been pointed out that the *arhat* is the ideal saint of Theravada, while the *bodhisattva* type belongs to Mahayana. In fact, both types of sanctity overlap. To Western eyes, the *arhat* is the stoic, outer-worldly saint, while the *bodhisattva* is the committed, inner-worldly saint, intent upon alleviating the suffering condition of his fellowmen to such a degree that he vows to forego final bliss until all have been saved. There are countless mythical *bodhisattvas.* Perhaps the better known of them is Avalokitesvara who rescues people from evil passions, shipwrecks and demons; who grants children to the childless; who is the father-mother saint, glorified as Kannon, the Goddess of Mercy. Such are the celestial patron saints of earthly saints.

Saints are celebrated for their amity and compassion, their joy and humour, their agapeic love, spiritual powers, and indifference to worldly conditions, their chastity and for a plethora of other virtues.

3. HOLINESS, SECULAR AND MONASTIC

As Buddhist sanctity is the final goal of all beings, no one need eternally be lost, even though this sanctity is not attained in the present life. Yet all beings are not equally close to that goal because they are unequally disposed by their *karma.* This fact is appropriately illustrated from a comparison between the holiness of the laity and that of the monk.

(a) Laity: the holiness of householders

The possibilities for holiness open to the laity are fairly grim. We are told, in a variety of texts, that the homelife is full of impediments to sanctity, and that the layman will never obtain the supreme wisdom by living the detested life of a family man, by enjoying the pleasures of the senses which have him hanker after wife and children. For all that, we are well documented on the elements of a saintly life for the laity. Much like

Confucianism, Buddhism stresses good inter-personal relations as essential to spiritual growth: between parents and children, pupils and teachers, husband and wife, friend and friend, master and servant, laity and monk.

The Buddhist laity, often in a kind of initiation, express faith in the Three Jewels, i.e., the Buddha, his Law, and his Community. They also promise fidelity to the Five Precepts, already mentioned, the observance of which varies considerably according to time and place. There are special counsels for girls and wives. The ideal wife, the Buddha said, 'respects her husband, has no wishes of her own, no ill-feelings, no resentment, and always tries to make him happy'. (*Anguttaranikāya,* 4:197).

Buddhism has always known a high number of saintly mavericks, such as the *arhats* of India and the *hijiris* of Japan. In Mahayana there is another type of popular saint, often a layperson, which has recently come in for renewed attention even at universities. I refer to the *myokonin,* those 'wonderful good people' (as D. T. Suzuki calls them) whose *joie de vivre* is the measure of their inner freedom and ecstatic trust in Amida, their Saviour. *Myokonin* are marvellously integrated people whose character traits remind us of the Christian fruits of the Spirit. They are tolerant, compassionate, humble, poor and detached, pure and modest, generous and gentle, full of wonderment, joy and awe at the marvellous goodness of Amida. Their recent popularity, I submit, is due in part to the quest for models of an uninhibited and unpretentious spirituality, for a Buddhism with a human face. Their spirituality goes back to the earliest Buddhism which holds that all beings can be *bodhisattvas* provided, in the pungent words of Suzuki, 'they do not philosophise about the world's tribulations from a celestial abode'.

(b) Monks and nuns: the holiness of homeless brothers and sisters

The Buddha scored a stroke of genius when he incarnated his ideal of holiness in the fourfold community of mendicant monks and nuns, lay brothers and lay sisters, all of them dedicated professionally to the pursuit of salvation. Not long after his death, however, the ideal of perfection was often arrowed to the Orders of monks and nuns. Their life is still regulated by minute rules. From the earliest times they were enjoined to sanctify every act no matter how trivial it might be: 'In looking forward, or in looking round; in stretching forth or drawing in his arm; in eating, drinking, masticating or swallowing, sleeping or walking, in obeying the calls of nature, in going, standing, sitting, speaking or keeping still, the monk remains aware of all that this means, and he becomes mindful and self-possessed.' (*Dīgha-nikāya,* 2:65). The Rules of Discipline are recited in chapter. Offenses are confessed and appropriate penances are given.

Four offences warrant expulsion from the Order: fornication, theft, murder, and false spiritual claims.

A word must be said about celibacy. In early Buddhism celibacy was strictly enforced for monks and nuns. It still is observed in general, with the age-old exception of Japan where unmarried monks are very rare while the nuns live a celibate life. The Buddha's blunt advice in the matter has been preserved: 'O monks, you should not see women. Should you have to see them, refrain from talking to them. Should you have to talk, reflect: I am now a homeless mendicant. In the world of sin, I must behave like the lotus flower whose purity is not defiled by the mud'. (*Sūtra of Forty-two Sections*). Obviously, the practice of celibacy had to contend with all the obstacles raised by human nature and society. But the ideal remained alive, and even in today's Japan there is a renewed interest in a way of life which, centuries ago, the Buddha identified as practically essential to salvation.

The Order of nuns never flourished. At least in Japan, nuns (and monks) show little sense of vocation, and it is said that many enter the Order for reasons of convenience.

4. PROFILES OF BUDDHIST SAINTS

Saints participate in the awe and fascination of the divine. The historical holy man or woman, even during his lifetime may be recognised as such, and even worshipped. Buddhists, much like Christians, have their *sensus fidei,* that uncanny, intuitive perception of outstanding qualities which are the hallmark of a saintly life. For all that, each saint remains an individual who must be seen standing before the motley canvas of his time. Here follow half a dozen thumbnail sketches which may help the reader paint for himself the composite portrait of the Buddhist saint.

1. *Tu-shun* (557-640), many authors hold, is the nominal founder of the influential Hua-yen sect in China, still flourishing in Korea and Japan. At sixteen he became a monk. At an early age, he led in prayer and meditation, feeding a thousand people when there was only enough food for half of them. He cleared a mountain from infesting insects which promptly left at his command. He cured the deaf and the dumb, as well as a man possessed by an evil dragon who said through the man's mouth: 'The great Ch'an master has come; I can no longer stay!' He wielded the miraculous powers of shamans, both male and female. His was a compassionate nature extending love to all without distinction. Hence he gained the respect of all, monks and laity, noble and mean. In imitation of the Buddha, he remained unperturbed in the face of praise and censure.

Once when he crossed a river and had to pull up the hem of his garment, he fell back into the water. Suddenly the water stopped flowing and allowed him to reach the other shore without wetting his feet, only to start flowing again when he was safely on land. At the age of eighty-four he sat upright in meditation and passed away without having been sick. He was buried in a sitting position and placed in a hole. The place was filled with fragrant odors. People built a shrine above the grave. (*Taisho Edition of the Buddhist Tripitala,* vol. 50, p. 653-4).

2. *Gyogi* (670-749) had a charismatic personality attracting thousands of people who recognised his divine powers and called him *bodhisattva,* a title posthumously confirmed by the Emperor for the first time in Japan. Gyogi was a wonder-worker, the ideal *hijiri,* a holy man, a true shaman possessing mediatory powers at the service of common people. He founded charity hospitals, orphanages, old people's homes; he dug canals and built bridges. His many projects were managed by disciples, monks and nuns as well as laity who lived in small communities nearby. The Emperor, who needed his help, elevated Gyogi who had no ecclesiastical training, to the rank of Archbishop. He died at the age of eighty, leaving behind more than 3,000 disciples.

3. *Kukai* (774-835) or Kobo Daishi was born in an aristocratic family. Legend mentions that his mother conceived after dreaming that an Indian monk entered her bosom, and that her pregnancy lasted twelve months. Kukai went to China. Hui-kuo, the master who received him exclaimed: 'I knew in advance that you were coming; we have awaited each other for a long time!' In 824 there was a severe drought. The Emperor ordered Kukai to come to court and pray for rain. He performed the appropriate rites, set the rain dragon free which his competitor had put in a bottle, and obtained abundant rain. He prophesised the moment of his death, refused the nectar brought to him by a celestial cook, and breathed his last. For ninety-nine days during which funeral rites were performed, his hair continued to grow and his body remained warm. Legend says that he did not die. His tomb is a popular place of pilgrimage on Mount Koya whence he shall come forth again to save all suffering people.

4. *Genshin* (942-1017) is a venerated founder of Japan's Pure Land tradition. Like Kukai, Genshin was a great artist and writer. He had a deep awareness of his *bodhisattva* vocation and said of himself: 'I formerly was a Buddha and I appeared in this world. Now that the conditions for salvation of others have been fulfilled, I shall return to my paradise.' Genshin became the father of many aspirants to holiness and of hundreds

of *communautés de base* whose influence upon Japanese religiosity remains even today his signal gift to the nation.

5. *Honen* (1133-1212), a disciple of Genshin, is affectionately known in the Western world as 'the Buddhist saint'. He was an articulate reformer, proclaiming 'the easy way to salvation'. He met with jealousy and persecution at the hands of the traditional sects. He was stripped of his monastic rank and banished from Kyoto. His 'easy way' brought salvation within immediate reach of the people and became a new source for social cohesion in the face of ecclesiastical oppression. About his deathbed there appeared purple clouds, while sweet music and various perfumes filled the room.

6. *Shinran* (1173-1262) is one of the most remarkable reformers Japan has ever known. His mother, one tradition says, requested that he become a monk on her deathbed. At Mount Hiei, Shinran became profoundly attached to Honen to the point that he wrote: 'There is nothing for me to do than to believe Honen. Even though I should go to hell because I was deceived by him, I should not regret it!' Shinran completed the process of declergification begun by Honen stressing that praise of Amida or the *nembutsu* was sufficient for salvation. At the age of twenty-one Shinran felt obsessed at the thought of his sins and passions. During a retreat he had a vision of the saintly Prince Regent, Shotoku Taishi, who appeared to him as Kannon Bosatsu promising to transform himself into a woman whom Shinran would embrace. Eshinni, who became Shinran's wife, confirms this tradition which suggests the difficulties of the celibate life.

At the time of his exile as a layman, Shinran found himself in a new society ready to receive his doctrine of pure grace for all, clergy and laity, men and women, on an equal basis of Amida's mercy. His spirituality was not a concession to the flesh but the cry of his faith. Totally evil man is totally dependent on the saving powers of Another. This called for a revolutionary style of life, different from that of the traditional monk. Shinran described his new life in these poignant words: 'I am an ordinary mortal, full of passions and desires, living in this transient world like the dweller in a house on fire.'

The pendant of total sinfulness is total redemption. According to Shinran, the Buddha nature and human nature are one and the same; saviour and saved are one; there is neither saint nor sinner. This is the famous doctrine of *kiho-ittai,* which teaches that Amida's saving vow transports the trustful sinner into an irreversible state of holiness. Thus the transcendent becomes the immanent as worldly bonds are divinised: 'All sentient beings in some birth or life have been my parents or my brothers. We can save them all when we become Buddhas in the life to come.' Shinran's death at eighty-nine was uneventful and yet classic. He lay on his right side with his head toward the north and his face toward the west. When he could no longer be heard reciting the name of Amida, he had passed away, thereby to be born unto Reality.

5. WHO IS A SAINT? WHY BUDDHIST SAINTS?

Holiness exhibits to the world the numinous dimension of religion, as Scripture states: 'Do not call the Tathagata by his name, nor address him as "friend", for he is the Buddha, the Holy One' (*Mahavagga,* 1:6). Buddhist saints are not the creation of a God, even though the Buddha is their creative ideal of perfection. In Buddhism and Hinduism the line between gods and saints is blurred. Historical saints are mythologised; mythological saints are historicised—a common religious phenomenon. Popular devotion, however, claims the privilege of humanising all saints before it divinises them. This reflects the anthropomorphic character of all sanctity and expresses the age-old belief that some mysteriously redeeming power penetrates the depths of this transient world. When this penetration becomes compenetration, as is the case in Mahayana, then, as H. von Glasenapp writes, 'it may be said that Buddhism in spite of all doctrinal differences is nevertheless based on the same assumptions, feelings and hopes as the theistic religions' (*Buddhism, A Non-theistic Religion* (London 1970) p. 125).

I have described the polyvalence of Buddhist sanctity: our saints are priests and prophets, healers and magicians. They are identifiable not so much by the similarity of their common goal but by the diversity of their ministries to a suffering world. Saints are archetypes which impress, influence and fascinate. They fill a deep socio-psychological and religious need, and 'they are responsible for the anthropomorphism of all God-images' (C. G. Jung *Collected Works* (London 1964) X, p. 449).

The Buddhist appointment with sanctity shows remarkable similarities to that in other religions. The last word on sanctity is not spoken in the normal course of life, but after death when the phenomenon can be completely grasped. Saints, somehow, are such by popular acclaim, which is an intuitive reaction of a community of believers, and therefore takes time. Officialdom, as we have seen, can be a help or a hindrance in fostering that reaction. But the final word belongs to the people who project their own spiritual aspirations upon the heroes of their choice. The phenomenological aspect of Buddhist sanctity, therefore, is popularity.

Are Buddhist saints necessary at all? They are not needed for creation, perhaps not even for salvation, at least in primitive Buddhism. But they do inspire people to yearn for perfection. Through vicarious experience Buddhist saints enrich our understanding of ourselves and of our world. Many of them, like Shinran, dramatise the tragic aspects of human life, as well as its nobility. Through them a tangible religious axiology becomes a living reality in our midst. Buddhism is inconceivable without the Buddha and its saints, and the seriousness of their quest for sanctity as the interpenetration of transcendent reality becomes the measure of its success as a full-scale religion.

Let Buddhist saints be wreathed in legends and mythology. When all embellishments are stripped away, they still remain the eloquent and often effective symbols of man's higher potentialities. With Pascal they know that, in man, there is more than man. The word 'saint' is adjectival, not nounal. The saint is not a god, but god-like, divine and deified. Yet he must stand before the judgement bar of human good because Buddhism concentrates on disciplining man's passions and channeling his emotions into the path of perfection. The Buddhist saint shares with us an internal humanism that puts the ultimate value of man in man himself. Thereby he serves as a corrector to the external humanisms of the West which are primarily concerned with man's outside world. Buddhist saints invite us to make our inner life more perfect, more compassionate, and more universal.

Buddhist saints then are not strangers in our Father's home. There are no hyphenated Buddhist saints, marginal or unimportant from the Christian point of view. In the eyes of millions of people, Buddhist saints possess awesome and beatifying powers which history proves may both reject and attract. They are never mere theoreticians or aestheticists. Even though they deny the existence of the self, they take the existence of the True Self most seriously, Buddhists saints, I feel, would agree with this statement: 'Where serious concern for self and open-hearted detachment from self coincide, access is thrown open to the holy. This, however, does not force the holy to appear. It gives itself only as a free gift' of Amida. (Karl Rahner, ed. *Sacramentum Mundi* (New York 1969) vol. 3, p. 52).

Meanwhile, we who are so insistent on historical accuracy and objectivity applaud the majestic saying of St Ambrose that 'whatever is good and lovely, by whomever it might have been said, comes from the Holy Spirit'. And we firmly believe that 'great holiness exists outside the Christian Church'. (Vatican II *Lumen Gentium,* 15).

Fernando Urbina

Models of Priestly Holiness: A Bibliographical Review

THE OBJECT of this article is to describe certain 'models of priestly holiness' in twentieth century Catholicism, with particular attention to a selection of texts. The concept of 'model' is used in a fairly imprecise way with no claim to an exact epistemological definition. It is synonymous with 'form', 'type', 'ideal'.

We shall begin by indicating the inevitable methodological limitations of this study. As Gabriel le Bras[1] remarks, Catholicism has important local differences within its common culture. Roughly speaking we can divide it into the 'Latin' (French-speaking Belgium, Latin Switzerland, France, Italy, Portugal, Latin America, Spain . . .); the Anglo-Saxon (England, Ireland—with its special influence upon the US—USA, Canada—where there is an admixture of the Latin tradition—and other countries with this culture). There is the Germanic sector which spreads out towards Scandinavia. And of special importance today there is the Catholicism of East Asia, Africa, India, the Philippines, Japan, etc. A limitation of which we are critically aware is that the models propounded in this essay are seen from within the Latin tradition. Elsewhere they might be different.

We attempt to compensate for this limitation, however, by the breadth of our basic schema: three important situations, stages or rhythms in a process which appears to have affected the whole Church, even though with variations. We are not going to defend this schema as our point of reference, as we have done so elsewhere[2] and its reality is fairly plain to any interested observer.

1. FIRST MODELS: THE RESTORATION OF 'CLASSICAL SPIRITUALITY', OR MORE ACCURATELY 'BAROQUE' BECAUSE IT DEVELOPED IN THE POST-TRIDENTINE PERIOD

Although the restoration of 'Catholic spirituality' began with the post-revolutionary restoration and was ideologically identified with it, here we limit our study to the twentieth century (with a few references to previous literature). From the beginning of the century there was a search for a spiritual model with a firmer theological foundation which set a high value on contemplation, including the mystical. France and Germany were the chief contributors. Let us briefly note some of its chief points.

1. *Popularisation of the contemplative tradition.* Poulain *Des Graces d'oraison* (Paris 1903); J. Tissot *La vida interior* (Barcelona 1935); Sauvé *La intimidad con Dios* (Barcelona 1933); Vital Lehodey *El Santo Abandono* (Barcelona 1926); D. J. B. Chautard *El alma de todo apostolado* (Buenos Aires 1935); and especially for a younger readership: *Arami Vivre* (Bonne Presse, Averbode, Belgium 1937). This is an odd publication with symbolic illustrations which are a mixture of 'lithographs of the life of Jesus' and *fin de siecle* symbolism—and the 'ideals of the good scout'.

It is a recommendation of the life of grace in the hearty terms of the thirties' youth movements (which were sometimes para-fascist). Fundamental to all this literature is a deep split between supernatural and natural life with a very negative attitude to the latter. This split could not be healed until Vatican II reaffirmed the historical unity of the history of salvation in theology.

2. *A Christocentric spirituality more firmly based on the Pauline theology of 'living in Christ'.* This superceded the pietistic devotions of the 'Sacred Heart' and the 'Lives of Jesus'. We select some of the more widely read works: D. Columba Marmion *Jesucristo Vida del Alma* (Barcelona 1936); the simpler works of P. Plus; a more theologically vigourous work: Karl Adam *The Son of God* (London 1934); Romano Guardini *The Lord* (London 1965).

3. *Liturgical spirituality* began its renewal with the work of Dom Guéranger *Institutions Liturgiques* 1840-1851; *L'année liturgique* 1841-1866. Later on, into the twentieth century, the Maria Laach movement spread from Germany. During the twenties and thirties the use of the Lefébure missal became popular among an élite of the laity. During the forties seminaries began to use the Bible and the liturgy for meditation instead of the Ignatian Exercises: Baur *Sed Luz* (Freiburg 1936).

4. *There are abundant ascetic elements* in an excessively voluntarist trend (which is sometimes balanced by the rediscovery of contemplation

and liturgy). In general this voluntarism is deeply impregnated with a negative attitude to the world, the body and sexuality. Typical books of this kind are: Hoornaert *El combate de la pureza* (Santander 1938); Tihamer Toth *Energía y pureza* (Madrid 1942). This book was extremely popular in religious colleges, seminaries and noviciates during the forties in the repressive atmosphere of Franco's Spain. Looking back we can say that great damage was done by this mixture of angeloid idealism, fascist voluntarism and pathological horror of human sexuality.

5. *A strong emphasis on the idea of 'sacrifice'* which, on analysis, reveals a complex of very ambiguous elements: (*a*) an evangelical component of generosity and self-giving; (*b*) in specifically priestly spiritual circles, priesthood was reduced to the idea of 'sacrifice' following the tradition of the French school; (*c*) a tendency to feel 'victimised' which began in the middle of the nineteenth century when the Western world was becoming irreversibly secular and Pius IX's Church rejected this world and adopted a 'state of siege'. Many new orders sprang up dedicated to 'expiation and reparation' and 'victimalist' ideas: Max Schmidt *Le anime vittime* (Rome 1931) (original German edition 1881). They felt the need to make reparation for a world absolutely dominated by evil; (*d*) Adolescents were offered angeloid ideals of 'teenage saints who died in the prime of their youth': St Thérèsa of Lisieux, St John Berchmans, St Stanislaus Kostka, St Luis Gonzaga, and this produced a psychoanalytically dangerous fascination in young people going through the difficult period of adolescence when confidence in the value of life was not yet firmly established, especially in closed institutions such as seminaries and noviciates. In many cases this 'victimalist and angelical idealism' ended literally in premature death.

6. *From these trends in spirituality a specific model of priestly holiness was constructed.* This model was nourished by reading certain works which were usually fairly weak in theological content and whose basic axiom was the 'holiness required for the dignity' of the priesthood, followed by ascetic advice which usually had a negative attitude towards the world: Bouchage *Vie sacerdotale* (Paris 1879); Cardinal Manning *The Eternal Priesthood* (London, Burns and Oates, undated, approx. 1885); Dubois *El sacerdote santo* (Madrid 1951); Cardinal Schuster *Ministerio Parroquial* (addressed to parish priests) (Buenos Aires 1941) etc.

From Belgium came the theologically and spiritually valuable work of Cardinal Mercier *La Vida Interior. Lamamiento a las almas sacerdotales* (Barcelona 1940, 1st edition Malines 1918).

Two works on the priestly vocation were influenced for very different reasons: Cardinal Mercier *A mes séminaristes* (Louvain 1932, 1st edition 1913) and Lahitton *La vocation sacerdotale* (Paris 1908).

Mercier's great work should be seen in the context of the post-

Tridentine tradition which attempted to construct a more coherent 'model of priestly holiness'. The tradition included Brémond, the French school originating with Bérulle, Condren, Olier, St John Eudes . . . certain elements in the Italian tradition (Borromeo) and the Spanish (Ignatius). This model was offered in seminaries devoted to the model of the 'village priest'[3]: Trochu *Vida del Cura de Ars* (Barcelona 1942).

Let us now summarise some of the characteristics of the ideal of holiness of this period, which was nourished by the works we have quoted and founded on a tradition going back to the seventeenth century, the high baroque:

(a) *affirmation of the primacy of religious, sacral values* (derived from Bérulle's theocentricism via S. Sulpice);

(b) *recommendation and demand for the contemplative life:* 'prayer the soul of every apostolate' but the medieval monastic formula *'contemplata aliis tradere'* was not sufficiently balanced by the much richer, more dialectic Ignation tradition of *'contemplativi in actione'*;

(c) *values of sacrifice and generosity,* but sometimes there is no clear demarcation of the boundary between evangelical loving sacrifice and masochistic self-destruction, because of the extremely negative attitude towards the world;

(d) *an asceticism which formed strong characters* but which sometimes tended towards a voluntarism accompanied by a mental rigidity in adolescents trained in a schematic philosophy: neo-scholasticism. This strict mental dogmatism, with its Olympian ignoring of the huge changes that had taken place in modern thought created priests who, instead of being trained to 'ask and listen in dialogue', knew all the answers in advance;

(e) *basic lack of a theological foundation* truly consistent with the fundamentals (*norma normans*) of the New Testament. The basic axiom derives the 'exalted holiness' of the priest from his 'high dignity' by a linear logical argument beginning with the supreme dignity of the priestly function among the ancients (pagans and Jews) and concluding *'a fortiori'* with the even higher dignity of those who hold 'power' over the 'physical body' and the 'mystical body'. In its definition of the ministry of the Church, this argument frequently applies (with no critical exegesis) the passage from *Hebrews* in which the author describes the high priest of the cult abolished by Christ.[4] This is a fundamental theological error which was seriously criticised in what we have called our 'third period'.

In fact Jesus Christ does not stand in linear continuity (although uniquely superior) to the Levitical (or pagan) priesthood. In the relations between God and the human race the Gospel event is an *essential rupture*. The office of priesthood is no longer tied to a sacral power connected with a space separated off from the people and with the social power. The ontological, existential and social change is decisive. The word 'hierus' is not used in the New Testament. It is replaced by the term 'diakonia'. The concept is radically altered. Priesthood is not seen as power to dominate but as a ministry of service. The 'words of service' given at the Last Supper are the institutional foundation of the Church.[5] A tragic misunderstanding led to the translation of the *exousia* of the Spirit by the concept of *auctoritas* and *potestas* of imperial Roman law. The consequences of this misunderstanding for the baroque 'model of holiness' (which prolonged the idealisation of the socio-historical structure of the ministry in the Middle Ages) were enormous, especially in the practical existential and social sphere. Here we cannot go deeply into this serious problem, but merely indicate it.

The cause of this theological-spiritual misunderstanding lay in a perhaps inevitable socio-historical contamination when the 'Church as Sacrament' became the 'Church as Empire'.[6] The ministry became the government of the *Corpus Christianorum* which historically identified the Church with the body politic of christendom. The ideological basis for this was the work of the fifth century neo-platonist philosopher Denis the Areopagite. His concept of the priesthood expressed perfectly the verticalist ideology of 'orders' current in archaic agrarian medieval society,[7] through the isomorphism of the angelic hierarchy (cosmic hierarchy of heavenly spheres) = vertical social hierarchy = also vertical ecclesial hierarchy: 'sacred' priests at the top, then monks, and lastly the laity. . . . The priest, who was ontologically superior in the sacral order, influenced the people 'from above downwards', by purifying, enlightening and sanctifying them. This basic ideological schema, present in the Thomist synthesis,[8] was reactivated in the great baroque spirituality of Bérulle and the French School.[9] Its influence, restored outside its historical context, continued in the model presented by the Catholic restoration of the nineteenth and twentieth centuries. This lasted until the decisive change to the 'Second Model' effected by Vatican II.

This model maintained the Levitical dichotomy between the sacred and profane which had been overcome once and for all in the eschatological transcendentalisation of the divine presence throughout the human universe.[10] As a result of this, the figure of the minister of the Church was over-sacralised and separated from the 'profane' life of the people, their love and work and social and cultural activities. . . .

From the time of Pius IX onwards this ideologico-existential system became institutionalised and the natural context for this 'model of priestly holiness' was the Church in a state of siege, which attempted to prolong a 'parallel self-enclosed space', the anachronism of baroque Christianity which had historically ceased to exist in modern secular society. In this ghetto the language of modern thought was banned and the ministry used the anachronistic language of neo-Thomism, which was inadequate to deal with modern life, science and thought. Once communication had broken down there could be no missionary dialogue. It was possible to preach to the archaic agrarian peoples of Africa but not to the workers of Clichy or Vallecas. This 'dominant separation of the sacral figure of the priest' created enormous difficulties when the time came for the laity to be integrated into the active life of the Church and take real responsibility.

A reductionist interpretation of the declarations of the Council of Trent, Sess. 23, which had a very specific historical cause,[11] led spiritual masters to reduce the defining essence of the ministry to the identity: priest = sacrifice, which was the foundation of the French priestly spirituality that had the results mentioned above.

To sum up: *ultima ratio* which appears to underlie the construction of this ideological system is the idea of the 'sacral separation of the priest' which had a non-Christian origin. Jesus of Nazareth did not choose to cut himself off from sinners and outcasts, as did the monks of Qumram. He ate and drank with publicans and sinners. The gospel model of holiness is not one of separation but of universal communion. There is no difference or ontological superiority between the 'state of ministers' and the 'state of common believers' in the community of the people of God.[12] Thus *the best definition of the minister of the Christian Church* is the one given by Fr Foucauld: he is *everyone's brother.*

2. SECOND MODEL OF PRIESTLY HOLINESS: A PRIEST FOR A CHURCH IN A STATE OF MISSION

First we shall point out schematically certain aspects of this model's spirituality, with a selection of the literature in which it was expressed.

1. *The discovery of 'human values'.* Sellmair *El Sacerdote en el mundo* (Madrid 1942). A much more profound work had a strong liberating influence in seminaries and noviciates: Ch. Moeller *Literatura del s. XX y christianismo* (Madrid 1960). This was a new look with love and understanding at literary work which reflected the quests, conflicts, real light and darkness of the modern world. The iron curtain which had separated the priest from the literature of his time was broken. Another crucial advance was the 'Copernican revolution' which healed the split between

supernatural and natural and rediscovered the fundamental unity of God's plan as both Creator and Redeemer. This was the work of Teilhard de Chardin published at his death by Editions du Seuil, Paris: *Le Phénomène humain* (1955), *Le Milieu divin* 1957 (English edition, London 1960).

2. *The discovery of the Church as a community through the experience of 'teamwork'.* In southern Latin countries (Italy, Spain, Portugal, Latin America) this was achieved by P. Lombardi's 'Movement for a better world' (see Lombardi *Esercitazioni per un mondo migliore* (Rome 1952). There was the movement for short courses in Christianity: *Cursilhos. Documentos basicos* (São Paulo 1974). There were Christian family groups but the most important of these movements was Catholic Action, especially the JOC with its programme of life revision: Maréchal *La revision de vida* (Barcelona 1966). Priests got over their separation and joined with other believers in dialogue about the faith of the community. This was a decisive step: Rétif *El equipo sacerdotal* (Salamanca 1967).

3. *Towards a spirituality which overcame categories like 'dignity', 'dominant separation', etc.* and rediscovered the gospel values of simplicity, incarnation and presence in the world of the poor etc . . . This trend was strongly influenced by the spirituality of the Little Brothers of Jesus. A fundamental book for this was: Voillaume *Au Coeur des Masses.* Other priests were offered as models: J. F. Six *Carlos de Foucauld. Itinerario espiritual* (Barcelona 1962). There was an attempt to rethink the theology and spirituality of the priesthood. G. Thils *Naturaleza y espiritualidad del clero diocesano* (Buenos Aires 1947).

4. But the strongest factor in the change of model was the powerful movement which transformed both the theory and the practice of the life of the Church. Nostalgia for a *Church of christendom* dissolved (Mounier *Feu la chretienté*) and the ideal was a *Church in a state of mission.* The centre for this historical transformation was France during the Second World War. See Louis Rétif *J'ai vu naitre l'Eglise de demain* (Paris 1971); a collection edited by Barauna *La Iglesia del Vaticano II* (Rio- Barcelona 1966).

We can sum up certain points about this new model: As against the affirmation of the dignity and quasi-ontological superiority of the 'priest' in a hierarchic scale of neo-platonic origin, as against 'consecration' as 'separation', there was a rediscovery of the essential structure underlying the new human relationship brought into the world by the Church, the sacrament of universal human communion: this structure is brotherhood: 'Can no man your father on earth, for you have one Father who is in heaven, and you are all brothers.' Matt. 23:8-10.

As against the negative attitude to human beings as the actually are here and now (rather than 'scholastic man' who lived during the thirteenth century), there arose (*Gaudium et Spes*) a readiness to meet these real people with their joys and woes, dramas, hopes, conflicts and limitations. There arose the idea of action, in the gospel sense, incarnation, involvement, mission.

As against the exlusive monopoly of the ecclesial attitude there was a rediscovery of the traditional truth (silenced during the baroque period) of the real priesthood of the people of God, which is the 'chief priesthood'—the other being 'ministerial', that is to say the priesthood is for ministry which means service.

3. THIRD STAGE. CRISIS, DEEPENING, BROADENING OF THE SECOND MODEL OF THE MINISTRY FOR A CHURCH IN A STATE OF MISSION

Since about 1968, parallel to the 'crisis of civilisation', there seems to have been a growing state of bewilderment among priests. This has been called the 'priest's identity crisis'. There is a large literature attempting, (*a*) to diagnose the situation, (*b*) to find a more solid theological and spiritual foundation. Here are some titles: Maurice Bellet *Crisis del Sacerdote* (Barcelona 1969). (The original title is more expressive: *La Peur ou la Foi* (Paris 1967); H. Küng *Why Priests?* (London 1972); Duclot-Lethielleux *Le prêtre: foi et contestation*; O. Gonzalez de Cardedal *Crisis de seminarios o crisis de sacerdotes?* (Madrid 1967); A. Andreu *Qué es ser cura hoy?* (Alcoy 1971); Salaün and Marcus *Qu'est-ce qu'un prêtre?* (Paris 1965); German Episcopal conference *El ministerio sacerdotal* (Salamanca 1970); Schillebeeckx *Sintesis teologico del sacerdocio* (Salamanca 1967); Ramon Prat *El sacerdot avui: vida y missió* (Barcelona based analysis of a universal crisis) (Barcelona 1969); J. Colson *Ministre de Jésus-Christ ou le sacerdoce de l'évangile* (Paris 1969); P. Grelot *Le ministère de la nouvelle alliance* (Paris 1967); Team led by J. Delorme *El ministerio y los ministerios segun el Nuevo Testamento* (Salamanca 1975) etc.

Possible causes of the crisis

First we must eliminate superficial 'spiritual' explanations (lack of ascesis, failure in devotion to Our Lady etc.) In fact the minimum of historical sense makes it impossible for us to idealise any age in the past. Empirical knowledge or eye-witness accounts of the dramatic situation of many priests during the 'baroque model' period, the severe psychological conflicts suffered by many priests in insoluble situations, because of an inhuman law which was contradictory to a society which claimed to support human dignity and rights, were intolerable. The clarification and the opening of ways out of dead-end positions which is happening now leads us to think that the authenticity and spiritual honesty of today is greater than in any idealised past. The causes of the crisis must be sought at deeper historical and theological levels.

The Church's 'state of siege' during the nineteenth and twentieth centuries up till Vatican II, was a citadel in which the 'baroque spiritual restoration' could artificially defend the priest's security with walls to shut him off from real human life and modern thought. But this situation was incompatible with the Church's essential missionary vocation. The choice was between the Church becoming a backwater or opening its gates to meet the outside world. Vatican II chose the latter. 'The windows were opened and a hurricane came in.' Whose fault was it? Four centuries of withdrawal and defence of dogmatic, ethical, theological and spiritual language which was meaningless and lifeless for ordinary people of the time. When the Spirit spoke it was very difficult to hear him. Great courage was needing to leap over the great chasm that yawned between the Church and history. . . .

The alternatives in this crisis were neatly named by Maurice Bellet in the title of his book: *El Miedo o la Esperanza* (*Fear or Hope*). The supporters of fear wanted to turn back to the anachronistic 'baroque model' (with rosary and cassock: the 'long dress' of courtiers to distinguish them from the peasants who wore short dress).

It is odd that in this moment of historical crisis and general insecurity the 'supporters' of this alternative are of course people who feel the greatest 'fear' of the crisis: the powerful and the rich. The re-restoration would have the same social significance as the nineteenth century restoration: a new pact between the Church and the conservative ruling classes. It would be another refusal to recognise the rights of the poor and those who are fighting for a better future and greater freedom. Let us hope that those in responsible positions will have the strength of faith and hope to understand that the 'second model, incarnate, involved, evangelical and missionary' corresponds best to a 'Church in a state of mission'. Let us hope that they see that the crisis can be overcome by a spiritual enrichment, the signs of which are alive and growing all over the world. Some books which note these signs of vitality: on the vigorous movement for local communities, see the bibliography in *Concilium* 104 (April 1975), on the 'movements of spiritual awakening', see *Concilium* 89 (November 1973). We could say that in some ways during this recent period the centre of spiritual creativity has shifted from the Old World to the young American countries. Thomas Merton's spiritual writings are very popular especially in his recent period of ecumenical discovery of oriental spirituality: *Thomas Merton on Zen* (London 1976); *The Way of Chuang Tzu* (London 1970). But above all it is the Latin American writers who have produced a magnificent synthesis between contemplative spirituality and real involvement in the world of the poor, e.g.

Arturo Paoli *Le persona, el mundo y Dios* (Buenos Aires 1970); *Dialogo de la liberacion* (Buenos Aires 1967); *El grito de la liberacion* (Salamanca 1977); Segundo Galilea *Espiritualidad de la liberacion* (photocopied lectures, Malaga 1974); several contributors to the edition of *Christus* no. 488 entitled 'Hacia una espiritualidad de la liberacion' (Mexico 1976); all Gustavo Gutierrez' work on the theology of liberation is marked by a deep spirituality; Ernesto Cardenal *Vida en el amor* (Buenos Aires 1970), English edition: *Love* (London 1974); *Salmos* (Salamanca 1975); *El evangelio en Solentiname* (Salamanca 1975).

A completely new 'model of the holy priest', impressively close to the life of Jesus of Nazareth, is the story of the young worker priest, the Spanish Chilean Joan Alsina, who lived as a worker, was deeply involved with the poor and also exercised his ministry as a priest. He died tragically as an outcast crushed by the princes of this world (*arkontes tou kosmou toutou* 1 Cor. 2:8). A biography with several authors: *Joan Alsina. Chile en el corazon* (Salamanca 1978).

On the evening of his death he left a brief script in his room which is discussed in the above mentioned book. It is one of the most impressive spiritual writings of modern times. His style is poetic and symbolic, reminiscent of Dostoïevsky, Simone Weil and St John of the Cross, and he gives us an insight into the supreme choice he is about to make. Like Jesus in Gethsemane, in an agony of fear but strengthened by the Spirit, instead of taking refuge in the Bishop's house, which he still had the chance to do, he decided to go out to where he knew arrest, torture and death awaited him.

Translated by Dinah Livingstone

Notes

1. G. le Bras *Etudes de sociologie religieuse* 2 (Paris 1953).
2. 'Secularizacion y vida sacerdotal' *Iglesia Viva* 21 (1969) 229-256; 'Formas vitales de realizar el ministerio sacerdotal' *Vocaciones* 47/48 (May/Sept. 1970); 'Significacion historico-theologica de la figura historica del ministerio del Barroco' in *Sacerdotes: crisis y construccion* (Madrid 1971) etc.
3. The proposal to make the Curé d'Ars patron of the secular clergy is an odd one: he had apparitions from the devil, an obsession against popular dances, a strange psychology traumatised by the religious persecution of the Revolution, and above all he led his life in an archaic rural milieu which no longer exists.
4. Heb. 5:1. Exegesis today sees this text a literal reference to the Jewish Old Testament High Priest, who has no theological connection with the ministry of the Church. The argument for the 'dignity of the priest' (in linear comparison with the Old Testament priest) can be found in Molina's classic work (1608) which had a

strong influence on baroque thought. The use of this text from *Hebrews* and this argument comes up again with Pius XI *Ad catholici sacerdotii* 20th December 1935 (subtitled 'Dignitas excelsa'). This theory is clearly opposed by the text from *Lumen Gentium* referred to in note 12.

5. Luke 22:24-7.

6. H. Fries 'Kirche als Imperium' in *Wandel des Kirchenbildes und dogmengeschichliche Entfaltung, Mysterium Salutis* 4/1.

7. Le Goff 'La societé des trois ordres (clerum, nobilitas, laboratores . . .)' *La civilisation de l'occident mediéval* (Paris 1967) p. 319. Baroque implied an 'aristocratic reaction' to the rising bourgeoisie. J. Tapies *Le Baroque* (Paris 1968); F. Braudel *La traición de la burgesia en el Mediterraneo . . . en tiempo de Felipe II* (Madrid) vol. 2 p. 99. Against this archaising world arose the revolution of modernity: Kuhn *The Copernican Revolution* (Harvard 1957); Gusdorf *La revolution galiléene* (Paris 1966); A. Koyré *From the closed world to the infinite universe* (Baltimore 1957). Mysteriously Bérulle who crystalised an archaic priestly model was also the 'spiritual father' of the gigantic figure in modern thought: Descartes . . .

8. *S. T. Suppl.* Q. 37, a. 2 ad 4. Cosmological conception in *SCG* III 78-87.

9. P. Cochois 'Le Cardinal Bérulle Jerarche Dyonisien' *Revue de l'histoire des religions* (1961) p. 75 ff; Depuy *Bérulle, une spiritualité de l'adoration*; J. Calgy *Le sacrifice dans l'école française de spiritualité* (Paris 1951) etc.

10. Jesus abolished the temple system. John 4:21-4; Matt. 27:51.

11. In reaction against protestantism the ministry of the word was not included in the 'definition' (in the semantic sense) of priesthood. (This was not done till Vatican II (LG 24-7; PO 4-6: the schema of the three ministries as against the single relationship of priest to sacrifice.))

12. *Lumen Gentium* n. 32 para. 2.

Contributors

JOSEP ROVIRA BELLOSO was born in Barcelona in 1926, graduated in law in 1948 and received his doctorate in theology at the Gregorian in 1956. He now teaches systematic theology at the University of Barcelona. His publications include: *Estudis per a un tractat de Déu* (1970); *Fe i libertat creadora* (1971); *L'Univers de la Fe* (1975) and *Trento, una Interpretación teológica* (1979), as well as contributions to several pastoral and theological reviews. He is part of a pastoral group responsible for the parish of Santa María de Gornal, in Hospitalet, near Barcelona.

PIERRE DELOOZ was born at Namur in Belgium in 1921, and is professor at Mons Catholic University College. He is also consultant to the Pro Mundi Vita International Centre for research and information in Brussels. His published work on the subject of this article includes: *Sociologie et canonisations* (The Hague 1969).

CHRISTIAN DOQUOC, OP, was born in 1926 in Nantes (France) and was ordained in 1953. He studied at the Dominican centre at Leysse in France and at the University of Fribourg in Switzerland, at the Saulchoir in France and at the Ecole Biblique in Jerusalem. He holds a diploma granted by the Ecole Biblique and a doctorate in theology and is at present teaching in the theological faculty at Lyons. He is a member of the editorial committee of the journal *Lumière et Vie*. His recent publications include: *L'Eglise et le progrès* and *Christologie I* and *II* (Paris 1972).

EDUARDO HOORNAERT was born in Bruges (Belgium) in 1930. He is a priest in the diocese of Bruges, but has been working since 1958 among the people in Recife (north-east Brazil) and teaching at the theological institute there. He has also taken part in the Commission set up to study Latin American Church History (CEHILA) from the point of view of liberation. His published works include the following: articles published since 1962 in the *Revista Eclesiástica Brasileira* (Petrópolis); *Verdadeira e Falsa Religião no Nordeste* (Salvador 1972); *Formação do Catolicismo Brasileiro 1500-1800* (Petrópolis 1978²); *Historia da Igreja no Brasil, Primeiro período* (Petrópolis 1979²), in co-operation with others.

RENÉ LAURENTIN was born in France in 1917. He is a professor of theology at Angers and has taught in Canada, the USA, Italy and Latin America. He is a member of the Roman Mariological Academy, vice-president of the French Society for Marian Studies and a correspondent for *Le Figaro*. Among his many publications are several studies of Mary, Vatican II and the synods of bishops, and works on Bernadette of Lourdes, Jesus and the temple, Thérèse of Lisieux, Catholic pente-costalism, and the ministry.

CLAUDIO LEONARDI was born in Sacco di Rovereto (Italy) in 1925. He teaches in the University of Florence, edits *Studi medievali* and is president of the Italian commission 'Corpus philosophorum Medii Aevi'. Intil 1973 he was on the editorial board of the theological review *Renovatio* (ed. G. Baget-Bozzo). He is interested in the Latin classics, high medieval hagiography and medieval and modern history of Christian tradition. In essays such as *Storia del Cristo storia del mondo* (1972) and *Christentum und Islam in der post-modernen Kultur* (1973) he has attempted a theological reflection upon history. He is joint editor of *Conciliorum Oecumenicorum Decreta* (Freiburg 1962, Bologna 1973).

BERNARD PLONGERON was ordained priest in Paris in 1964. He has taught at the universities of Strasbourg and Louvain and is now assistant professor at the Institut Catholique de Paris (Lettres et Théologie), director of research and a member of the national committee of the Centre National de la Recherche Scientifique.

Bernard Plongeron is a specialist in the history of religious attitudes in pre-revolutionary France and the present day. He has published over fifty articles in France and abroad, and several books, most recently *Le Christianisme populaire: Dossiers de l'histoire* (Paris 1976) and *La religion populaire: Approches historiques* (Paris 1976).

JOSEPH JOHN SPAE was born at Lochristi, Belgium, and studied orientalism and Buddhism at Leuven, Peking, Kyoto (Otani and Imperial University), and Columbia University, New York, where he obtained a doctorate in Far Eastern languages and philosophy. In 1961 he founded Oriens Institute for Religious Research in Tokyo. In 1972-1976 he served as Secretary General of Sodepax in Rome and Geneva. At present he is Consultor of the Vatican Secretariat for Non-Christians and Co-director (with Robert Schreiter) of the Chicago Institute for Theology and Culture, established in 1978, with special responsibility for Asia and Europe. His books include: *Itō Jinsai* (Peking 1948 and New York 1968); *Catholicism in Japan* (Tokyo 1967); *Nihonjin no mita Kirisutokyō* (with Suzuki Norihisa) (Tokyo 1968); *Japanese Religiosity* (Tokyo 1971).

FERNANDO URBINA was born in Murcia (Spain) in 1923. He began studying physics at Madrid University but left to enter the Madrid diocesan seminary where he was ordained in 1950. He has worked in rural and suburban parishes. He has been adviser for many years to the Latin American Seminary in Madrid, and has given many retreats for clergy and religious in Spain, Portugal, France, Latin America. He is professor of spiritual, pastoral and fundamental theology at the Madrid Seminary, the Faculty of Theology in Granada and Comillas (Madrid), the Instituto Superior de Pastoral and the Instituto Superior de Catequetica (Madrid). His publications include: *Persona Humana en S. Juan de la Cruz; Violenza en el mundo y en la Iglesia; Sacerdotes: crisis y construccion;* (together with a team of investigators) *Iglesia y Sociedad civil en Espana 1936-75*. At present he edits the review *Pastoral Misionera.*